How To Raise Your Child's Emotional Intelligence:

101 Ways To Bring Out The Best In Your Children & Yourself

Allen Nagy, Ph.D.
Geraldine Nagy, Ph.D.

Heartfelt Publications
Bastrop, Texas

How To Raise Your Child's Emotional Intelligence:
101 Ways To Bring Out The Best In Your Children and Yourself
Allen Nagy, Ph.D. and Geraldine Nagy, Ph.D.

Heartfelt Publications
P. O. Box 1090
Bastrop, Texas 78602
Tel: 1-888-892-7006   Fax: 512-332-0874
E-mail: heartfelt@ibm.net Web: www.heartfeltpublications.com

Publisher's -- Cataloging-In-Publication
(Provided by Quality Books, Inc.)

Nagy, Allen.
      How to raise your child's emotional intelligence : 101
ways to bring out the best in your children and yourself
/ Allen Nagy, Geraldine Nagy. -- 1st ed.
      p. cm.
      Includes bibliographical references.
      LCCN: 98-93321
      ISBN: 0-9664287-0-6
      1. Emotions in children. 2. Parenting. 3. Emotions and
cognition. 4. Emotions--Social aspects. I. Nagy,
Geraldine. II. Title.

    BF723.E6N34 1998   649'.1
                            QBI98-969

The images used herein were obtained from IMSI's MasterClips Collection,
1895 Francisco Blvd. East, San Rafael, CA 94901-5506, USA.

The Old Grandfather and His Grandson from *The Moral Intelligence of
Children* © Robert Coles, Random House.

Children as Contribution from *Winning Through Enlightenment* © Ron
Smothermon, M.D., Context Publications.

Printed in the United States of America

DEDICATION

We want to dedicate this book to the children of the world for their bravery and their ability to withstand the kaleidoscopic rate of change that confronts them daily in our society. We want to thank all of those people who have brought children into this world and, even in the midst of making mistakes, have had the courage to do the best they could. They have made this world a richer place. We want to thank our parents, Helen and Louie, and Elizabeth and Lando, who have given us so much of what we speak about within this book. Without their love we would not have the courage to share our ideas about children. Finally, we want to thank our son, Clint, who has taught us more about Emotional Intelligence, kindness, and integrity than any book, teacher, or professional experience that we may have had throughout the years.

CONTENTS

INTRODUCTION

101 WAYS TO BRING OUT THE BEST IN YOUR CHILDREN AND YOURSELF

Contents

Contents

Contents

ACKNOWLEDGMENTS

This book has been a labor of love for both of us. We have been inspired and helped by many people. A special thanks goes out to Ron Smothermon, M.D. Many of the ideas contained in this book can be attributed to Ron.

Sita and Bo Lozoff, of the Human Kindness Foundation, have been a marvelous pair of role models for us.

We also wish to thank our editors, Susan Luton and Nancy Gustafson, for their many helpful suggestions to the original manuscript.

Finally, we want to thank David Smith, who created the artwork for the cover, and who provided constant encouragement. David is one of those rare individuals who possesses both high IQ and high EQ.

Humanity grows more and more intelligent, yet there is clearly more trouble and less happiness daily. How can this be so? It is because intelligence is not the same thing as wisdom.

When a society misuses partial intelligence and ignores holistic wisdom, its people forget the benefits of a plain and natural life. Seduced by their desires, emotions, and egos, they become slaves to bodily demands, to luxuries, to power and unbalanced religion and psychological excuses. Then the reign of calamity and confusion begins.

Nonetheless, superior people can awaken during times of turmoil to lead others out of the mire. But how can the one liberate the many? By first liberating his own being. He does this not by elevating himself, but by lowering himself. He lowers himself to that which is simple, modest, true; integrating it into himself, he becomes a master of simplicity, modesty, truth.

Completely emancipated from his former false life, he discovers his original pure nature, which is the pure nature of the universe.

—Lao Tzu (2500 years ago)

INTRODUCTION

EMOTIONAL INTELLIGENCE: WHY IT MATTERS MORE THAN IQ

Within the last several years, a clear distinction has been made between the old concept of intelligence (IQ) and the relatively new concept of Emotional Intelligence (EQ). The idea of raising emotionally mature children has been around for a very long time, but it has taken the work of Daniel Goleman, in his book entitled *Emotional Intelligence,* to bring the concept into the realms of mainstream education and psychology. An increasingly large number of people are coming to believe that there is too much emphasis on academic achievement and not enough on the development of emotional skills. A rapid rise in juvenile violence, the problem of adult criminal behavior, and the presence of many current social ills are reflections of this lack of attention to Emotional Intelligence in our culture.

Research indicates that people with a high level of Emotional Intelligence are happier, more successful, more socially responsible, less addiction-prone, experience more job satisfaction, and have more harmony in their relationships than people with low Emotional Intelligence. Simultaneously, there's an increased awareness that people with a high intelligence quotient (IQ) don't necessarily live a life consistent with high ethical standards, marital harmony, effective parenting, kindness, honesty, or a high quality of existence. Knowledge of complex mathematical formulas or even advanced psychotherapy techniques, or the ability to learn such formulas and techniques easily and quickly, is not strongly related to a diminished capacity for criminal activity, the ability to manage stress and emotions, to communicate effectively, to be empathic, to enjoy positive self-regard, or to engage in sound decision-making.

Clearly, knowledge is not wisdom. Having a high IQ doesn't mean we are emotionally wise. Wisdom is the application of knowledge to our everyday lives. It isn't the academic knowledge of the head that makes us wise. It's the emotional knowledge of the heart and spirit that makes for wisdom. The evidence is now clearly pointing to the need for a "Heart Start" program as well as a "Head Start" program.

Almost every parent wants his child to be emotionally mature. Yet it's a rarity to find a parent who doesn't unnecessarily complicate the life of their children. And though there's a strong reluctance to admit these shortcomings, many parents psychologically turn away from their children as the latter grow older. In the interim, they confuse and alienate them endlessly. We don't have to do this any more!

EMOTIONAL INTELLIGENCE (EQ): WHAT IS IT?

The cornerstone of Emotional Intelligence is *empathy*. Empathy involves feeling—primarily feeling how other people feel. It's putting yourself in the position of the other person. One time many years ago when my son was a toddler, he and I were walking hand and hand through a crowded shopping mall during the Christmas holidays. He was lagging behind, clearly not having much fun, and was on the verge of tears. Several times I asked him what was wrong as I more or less pulled him down the busy aisles. I didn't get any verbal response to my questions, so finally I bent way down to the point where my eyes were on the same level as his eyes. Suddenly, I realized that all he could see from his level of the world was butts. Butts, butts, and more butts—and most were pretty much in his face as we progressed down the mall's aisles. As I saw things from his perspective, I could understand his feelings and feel with and for him. This is a case of empathy in "hindsight"—seeing things from the other person's perspective.

Emotional Intelligence also involves the awareness of our own feelings and our own thoughts. We're thinking almost all of the time, and we have feelings that correspond to these thoughts. For example, if I'm thinking that the man who is approaching me in a dark alley is going to rob me, I'm going to be afraid. Emotionally Intelligent people are aware of their thoughts and feelings and can adjust them according to the circumstances. This may sound simple, but it takes a great deal of learning and practice. It is generally a skill that we must be taught rather than something that we come by naturally. For the most part, we keep our minds so busily occupied with insignificant "thought chatter" throughout the day that we are unaware of our very own stream of thoughts.

If you ask a person to write down what he's been thinking during the last eight hours of his life, you would very likely get a puzzled look. Generally, people say they haven't been thinking very much at all and are able to report only a few specific threads of thought. But with just a small amount of practice most people can recall hundreds of thoughts and write down many pages of them in a "thought diary." People with healthy EQ's are aware of their thoughts as they arise; and they can monitor them for validity, thereby recognizing how much of what they feel results from what they are thinking.

In addition to being aware of the thoughts and feelings of others (empathy), and the thoughts and feelings they themselves are having (self-awareness), high EQ people have learned to manage their own emotions *and* can also manage the emotions of others in an effective way. In essence, they've learned to calm themselves during times of stress, as well as to also calm others who are experiencing emotional distress. Clearly, any person who is empathic, self-aware, skilled at handling his own emotions, and adept at assisting other people handle their emotions—such a person is going to be an excellent parental model for his children.

WHO THIS BOOK IS FOR!

With respect to Emotional Intelligence there are three categories of people. The first category is comprised of people who already have a high EQ. These people don't need the information in this book because they're already practicing it in the entire spectrum of their lives. Research suggests that about 25 percent of the population in the United States falls into this category. Despite the fact they don't "need" this information, I'm hopeful they'll read it and bring EQ into their lives and into the lives of the people they touch in a broader and more expanded way.

The next category of people are those who have a low level of EQ. It isn't likely that this group of people will take a serious interest in this book. I suspect that this group will become upset and angry when they hear about the EQ-raising practices that are being proposed. I hope that I'm in error, since my belief is that low EQ people comprise approximately 25 percent of our population. I actively welcome the opportunity to be proven wrong.

This book, I believe, can have its greatest impact upon the remaining 50 percent of our population. This large segment of people need and want inspiration and information. To some degree they are aware of the importance of EQ and are willing to put new child-rearing practices into effect. They have a desire to learn and to apply what they learn to their daily lives. It is my contention that the very existence of our society depends on the direction this group takes with respect to the development of their own EQ and with the quality of assistance they can provide to others. The development of this group's EQ level will become the foundation upon which the EQ of future generations is built. If you've read this far and are eager to hear more, that's a really good sign.

THE TEST

As of yet there is no truly valid test that can clearly spit out a number representing your Emotional Intelligence. I've seen a few brief tests made up of ten to fifteen questions in popular magazines, but most seem to miss the point to a large degree.

Even though we don't have a widely accepted test that can measure one's EQ, it is very important to know that you have a healthy EQ level before we go any further. The reason for this is that you can't give what you don't have! The Universe just won't allow it. You can't help someone else out of quicksand when you are waist-deep in quicksand yourself. You need to be firmly grounded in a healthy EQ foundation before you can promote it in others. As an individual who has practiced psychotherapy with clients for twenty years, it is clear to me that I can't take anyone any further than my own level of psychological health. I suspect that as parents, we can't take our children's EQ level much beyond our own. From this perspective, it is vitally important for parents to be working on the development of their own EQ. Unfortunately, our EQ does not automatically increase with the passing of each calendar year. EQ only increases with effort and practice.

Given the clear importance of having a healthy level of EQ before being able to assist others with their own EQ development, I'm going to propose a test to measure your EQ. Scientifically this test has no validity, but from the level of intuition it has a lot of "face validity."

The following excerpt is a brief chapter taken from the marvelous book *Winning Through Enlightenment* by Ron Smothermon, M.D. The chapter is entitled "Children as Contribution." The test instructions are to (1) read the following section *twice* and (2) answer the questions that follow.

Children as Contribution

"Let's clarify something about children. They have a lot to teach us and they are a lot of trouble. Let's face it; they wet their pants, cry in public, demand to be fed, question our beliefs, spend our money, waste our time, and you can finish this very long list. Nevertheless, people continue to have children. There is clearly more to children than pain.

Children bring us something from the other universe for which we hunger as much as we hunger for food. They bring a certain quality to life without which life would not be worth living. If suddenly there were no children in the world, we would then know the contribution our children make to our lives. They are a fresh embodiment of the Self, immediately caught in a physical form. They have not had time to adopt the worldly beliefs that so structure and limit our lives. To a child, not only is everything possible, everything is.

Now, because they are also a lot of trouble, we often do not acknowledge the contribution our children bring to our lives. We blind ourselves to who our children really are; a new embodiment of God, the Context of the universe. God will never speak to you so clearly as through your child's laughter or tears. A child has not had time to forget how to experience life directly. Consequently, your children will know more than they are supposed to know. At times you will feel grossly ignorant in the presence of their knowing.

So, I want you to know what is primary and what is not primary. I want you to know which context works with children: pain or contribution. I want you to know which context holds the *other, that is, which is senior and which is junior. Children are a magical contribution to our lives. Within this context of magical contribution is held that they are a pain and a lot of trouble. Therefore, acknowledge your children. Let them know what they contribute to your life. They know, but they don't know that you know, and they **want** to know that you know. It makes their lives worth living. Like you, they are here for the purpose of serving and being served by others, and they know it. Children make you a family. Without them, we are merely relationship. When they come into our lives we are family. Let them know that they make your life worthwhile. If you do, they will maintain their magical quality all of their lives and you will have them as friends in later years. If you don't, you endarken the world, for early in their lives children incorporate your thoughts, even your voice, into their minds. Don't burden the minds of your children with heavy, serious content."*

TEST QUESTIONS

Does this excerpt arouse strong feelings of love for your
    children?

YES_____ NO_____

Are you willing to go to your children now and tell them, from
    your heart, they make a valuable contribution to your life?

YES_____ NO_____

Are you open to the idea that you and your children are here
    on Earth for the purpose of serving and being served by
    others?

YES_____ NO_____

Are you committed to maintaining and bringing forth the
magical quality and decency of your children?

YES_____ NO_____

Do you see that God will never speak to you so clearly as
through your child's laughter or tears?

YES_____ NO_____

If you answered with a resounding YES to all five of these
questions, I suspect that you have a very healthy EQ level and
represent an excellent teacher/model for the development of EQ
in others. You're probably among the 25 percent that really don't
need this book (but I hope you continue onward anyway). If you
answered NO to two or more questions, I suspect that this book
will strongly challenge your current way of raising children. I hope
you continue onward also. Finally, if you were one of those people
who had one NO response and a few weak YES answers, please
forge ahead. The quality of your life, your children's lives, and
the very quality of humankind's future existence hangs in the balance. We must never forget the importance of children, for it is
they, more than any other factor, who must compel us to choose
love over hatred, peace over war.

WHAT LIES AHEAD?

What lies ahead are 101 suggestions on how to improve
your own EQ and the EQ level of others, especially your children. We have included our favorite quotes to bring these ideas
alive. When an author is not indicated, the quote is our own.

If you feel committed to raising the EQ of yourself and others, CONGRATULATIONS! This commitment may represent the
best test available anywhere to measure your current EQ level.

1

Make A Commitment To Increase The Number Of Emotionally Intelligent People On The Planet

In the Old Testament (Genesis), we are told that God was willing to forego the destruction of the world for the sake of ten righteous people. What would happen today if God applied the same standards to our world? Do ten truly righteous people exist? Perhaps we can substitute high Emotional Intelligence for righteousness. What would be our fate if God were willing to forego the destruction of the world for the sake of ten people with a high EQ? There's some very good news for us. According to research presented by Paul H. Ray (*Noetic Sciences Review,* Spring 1996), 24 percent of the people in the United States have a high concern for spirituality, ideals, psychological development, and the environment. These people are depicted as having a concern for developing healthy relationships and are open to the creation of a positive future. According to this research, there aren't just ten high EQ people, but forty-four million people with a high level of Emotional Intelligence. This is a fantastic start. This book is about increasing that number. It is about putting you in that category if you aren't already there. And most importantly, it is about providing you with 101 things you can do to ensure that your children grow up to be Emotionally Intelligent adults.

Perhaps the single most important thing you can do to increase your children's EQ is to work on increasing your own. In a literal sense, our role as parents is to serve our children. The way we behave, day in and day out, has a tremendous impact on our children. They see how much love we extend to others and, early on in life, they adopt a level of happiness, peacefulness, and respect for themselves and others that is very similar to the levels we demonstrate.

Work on increasing your EQ. It is a great gift to your children, to yourself, and to the world. Part of the beauty of this work is that you receive what you give. If you promote the EQ of others, your EQ grows in the process. Giving and receiving are truly the same.

We are living in a period of rapid-fire change in which the fate of humankind could easily slide in either a positive or negative direction. Make the commitment to social and spiritual responsibility. Do so by beginning in your own home with yourself, your family, and your children.

*We are all in this thing called Life together, and either we are **all** going to make it or **none** of us is going to make it. In a very real sense we are our brother's keeper. The generations of children to come deserve their chance at Life. We have the power to grant them this.*

2

Choose Love Over Conflict In Your Relationship With Your Children And Spouse

God's Little Instruction Book for Dad offers us the following quotation, attributed to Josh McDowell: "The greatest thing a father can do for his children is to love their mother." Perhaps it is also true that the greatest thing a mother can do for her children is to love their father. How successful are we in this regard? If the world could watch a videotape of the last ten hours of your interaction with your spouse, would you be proud of what they saw? How many acts of tenderness, kindness, and love would be revealed during that ten-hour video?

The world will never see that video, but your children will watch hundreds of real-life hours of such interaction. Are you proud of what they see? Clearly, a marvelous gift to give your children, and one that is sure to promote high EQ, is to choose love over conflict in your relationship with your spouse.

---

*While with an eye made
quiet by the power
of harmony, and the deep
power of joy,
We see into the life of things.*
—William Wordsworth

♥

These things I command you, that ye love one another.
—The Bible

3

Never Pass Up An Opportunity To Touch, Hold, Or Hug Your Children

Children need to be physically touched to be emotionally healthy. You may be aware of the often-cited research that found that young infants, even when their physical needs (such as food, water, shelter, warmth) were adequately provided, suffered grave physical ailments when their needs for love, physical touching, and human interaction were not being met. These children were not receiving emotional nourishment.

Such findings have been repeatedly documented with animal research. The young of almost every primate species need parental affection in order to develop normally—to have a healthy EQ. A fascinating article in *Time* (October 13, 1997) entitled "Young, Single, and Out of Control" discusses documented evidence that rhinos are being killed by young, aggressive bull elephants. It appears as though all the young elephants were orphans of parents killed or relocated during an operation designed to help establish a more healthy elephant population. The author of the article, Michael D. Lemonick, states, "Since 1987, almost 1500 orphan calves, 600 of them males, have been moved to unfamiliar locations and raised without exposure to adult elephants or the hierarchical social structure that defines elephant life." In essence, there are no older male elephants to act as role models for the young bulls, and it appears as though this lack of adult contact and supervision has created a generation of juvenile delinquents.

So be there for your children. Hold them, hug them, touch them, and never pass up an opportunity to do so. Occasionally, I've heard men express the fear that their son might not be masculine if they demonstrate a lot of physical affection. The opposite is true. Male children of "embracing" parents are judged to be more masculine than male children who are not physically embraced. This contact not only benefits our children but also satisfies our own deep-seated need to be spiritually connected with others.

and if ever i touched a
life i hope that life
knows
that i know that touch-
ing was and still is and
always will be the true
revolution.

—Nikki Giovanni

4

Tell Your Children You Love Them And Nurture Their Spirits

If you wish to be loved, love.
—Seneca

We all know that murder is the act of killing someone physically. A more common type of destruction is the killing of the spirit. We can see that the glow in the eyes of some children has been dimmed by harsh discipline, physical or verbal abuse, and a lack of respect for the child as a person. Nurture your child's spirit with love. Tell them you love them often, express your feelings openly, and promote the expression of their positive thoughts and feelings. That which isn't expressed will shrivel and die.

I once heard someone say, "Not one of us has received enough love." Make a loving commitment to your children so that this will not be true for them.

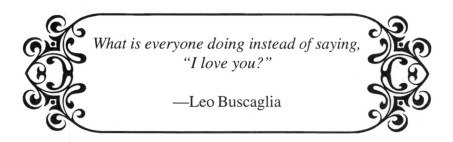

What is everyone doing instead of saying, "I love you?"

—Leo Buscaglia

5

Set Aside A Certain Period Everyday For Being With Each Of Your Children

Let your children know that this is their time to be with you and your time to be with them. Don't let anything interfere with this scheduled interaction time. Without formally declaring a time to be together, it's easy to get caught up in the hectic activities of daily life and forget that our children are primary to us. Our society is hardly an ideal place for raising children. Many families are single-parented or consist of two working parents. The extended family of grandparents and relatives is frequently not physically or psychologically available to assist with care-giving to the children. Meeting with your children at the designated time becomes habitual just like being on time for our job. If we can be on time for work every morning, we can certainly demonstrate the same level of reliability to our children. It also affords us the opportunity to demonstrate the concept of dependability.

☽☽☽

Time's most important quality is that it passes,
that we have only a finite amount.
Therefore, be aware of its value
and know that when you give your time
you're giving of your life.

—Daphne Rose Kingma

6

Keep Your Promises

It is vital to keep your word to your children. It's easy to make a promise without the intention of keeping it. The child wants to go to the park; we're tired and we say, "I'll take you tomorrow." We may be well-intended or we may just be hoping that the child will forget about the park trip the next day. If he doesn't forget and we make up some excuse for not going, we've broken our promise and the child will notice.

If this is a pattern, the child will also notice that a promise is not really a promise—*that it is not important to keep your word or do what you say you'll do.* Obviously, parents won't always feel like doing what they said they would do. Such occasions offer an excellent opportunity to model EQ. Tell your child, "I don't really feel like going to the park today, but I did promise and it's important to keep my word to you. I'm going to work at setting my feelings and thoughts aside, just like I ask you to do sometimes, and I think we can have a good time at the park."

In many respects, the quality of our relationships is directly related to our willingness to keep our agreements. In large measure, many of the problems we have in life are the result of broken agreements. Unfortunately, when most of us break an agreement (and get caught) we immediately make up some excuse or justification for our actions. Any time a "Broken Agreement → Get Caught → Have an Upset" sequence of events occurs, and is followed by a justification, you can bet that agreement will be broken again. However, if the person doesn't justify the behaviors, but instead acknowledges the wrongdoing and makes a verbal commitment to keep his word, then the infraction is much less likely to reoccur. For example, if a spouse has an affair (Big Broken Agreement), gets caught (Really BIG Upset), and justifies the behavior—"my spouse is not the person I married ten years ago!"—the unfaithful behavior will very likely continue. Any behavior that is justified will occur again. If, on the other hand, the unfaithful spouse doesn't justify the behavior but instead takes ownership of it and responsibility for it, there will not likely be a repeat performance.

The vital point here is that it is crucial to keep our agreements with our children and with others. This is the only way our children will be able to see that if they don't want a life full of upsets, they need to keep their agreements—every last one of them. Keeping agreements is a matter of integrity and a reflection of responsibility.

Always do what you say you are going to do. It is the glue and fiber that binds successful relationships.

—Jeffry A. Timmons

7

Show Care And Concern For All Living Things

Recognize that almost every interaction with your children is an opportunity to demonstrate your own emotional maturity and to assist with the development of theirs. It can be a situation as simple as removing a thorn from the paw of the family dog. To ask a young child how the dog felt is a request for empathic responding. Don't miss these small opportunities to develop appropriate thinking patterns and to model care and concern for all living things.

Even as a mother protects with
her life
Her child, her only child,
So with a boundless heart
Should one cherish all living
beings—
Radiating kindness over the entire
world.
     —The Buddha

Do all the good you can, by all the means you can, in all the ways you can, in all the places you can, all the times you can, to all the people you can, for as long as you can.

—John Wesley

8

TellYour Children They Are Fundamentally Kind, Loving, And Loveable People

Tell your children who they fundamentally are over and over. In many respects the real task of parenting is to tell children who they are when they forget. I had a very psychologically healthy therapist and friend call me once and say, "Please tell me three things you like about me, because I can't think of anything right now."

Essentially, she was asking me to tell her who she really was—a kind, warm, and compassionate human being dedicated to serving others. But she forgot! When your children are misbehaving, or feeling down, it's likely that they have forgotten, too. So it is vital to tell our children who they are so they develop a consistent positive image of themselves. If your child pets the cat gently, tell him, "That must feel nice to the kitty. You're a kind person, aren't you?" If the child pulls the cat's tail, you can say, "That doesn't feel very good to Mr. Kitty. You're a nice person, but that wasn't a very nice behavior."

Our children are never too old to be reminded of who it is they fundamentally are. My nineteen-year-old son went to the mall to buy clothes and struck it rich when he found a store that had $30.00 shirts on sale for $3.00. He bought fifteen of them, several of which were for his girlfriend, and one for a male friend. I was pleased and proud of him for thinking of others during an exciting shopping episode, and I told him he was a kind and considerate person for doing so. I could tell he liked the compliment. Don't we all?

And remember, we are never too old. I frequently visit my eighty-six-year-old father who is wheelchair-bound. Often when

I'm leaving he tells me, "You're a good man, son." Suddenly, I'm a fifty-three-year-old child who is all aglow. Tell your children who they are everyday, because sometimes they forget.

A marvelous little exercise to do when you catch your children making negative comments about themselves ("I can't do anything," "I'm ugly," "I'm stupid," etc.) is to tell them, "What you just said is simply a thought and it isn't the deepest truth about you. The deepest truth about you is that you are kind, loving, and loveable." You can also do this as a planned exercise by asking your children to state something they don't like about themselves and then tell them that what they said is just a thought and not significantly related to who they fundamentally are. This practice also works well when something negative is said about others. In this case, you tell the child this is not the deepest truth about the other person.

Neither a lofty degree of intelligence nor imagination
nor both together go to the making of genius.
Love, love, love, that is the soul of genius.

—Wolfgang Mozart

9

Persistence And Determination Lie At The Heart Of EQ

Let your children know by both your word and your deed that "Nothing in the world can take the place of persistence. Talent will not; nothing is more common than unsuccessful men with talent. Genius will not; unrewarded genius is almost a proverb. Education alone will not; the world is full of educated derelicts. Persistence and determination alone are omnipotent." (Author unknown.)

This quotation strikes at the heart of EQ versus IQ. Model it for your children, discuss it with them, and praise them when they persist in the face of obstacles.

Life is the perfect teacher. Life knows what courses we each need to graduate, and will keep providing us with the same homework until we understand each lesson completely. We are all going to graduate—we have no choice about that. When we graduate is our choice. And when we do graduate, it will be with honors. This is true for every last one of us.

10

Give Attention To Your Child's Positive Behaviors

Constantly express appreciation for appropriate behavior. Healthy children will often openly ask for you to watch them. Do so frequently. Children cannot tolerate a condition of no attention. Pay positive attention to them. If they can't get positive attention, they'll create situations whereby they get negative attention, because negative attention is preferable to no attention. Unfortunately, parents, teachers, and many systems within our society do the reverse. The child who gets the most attention in school isn't the quiet, well-mannered student but rather the one who is putting bubble gum in someone else's hair. Our children *will* get our attention—we don't have much choice about that. Our only choice is which behaviors will receive our attention. Pay heed to their appropriate behavior and acknowledge them for it. Then they won't feel the need to get attention by behaving negatively.

This same scenario, in some form, is also true for adults. As adults, we generally don't ask other people to look at us in the explicit way that children do, but we never really lose our need for approval and attention. As we "mature," our needs for attention and the ways we attempt to get it become less direct. Many of these attention needs are expressed in socially positive ways such as academic success, athletic skills, prestigious vocations, acquiring the stuff of which the American Dream is made. Or these attention needs can be expressed with facial tattoos, nose earrings, antisocial behavior, gang affiliations, infidelity, or bizarre psychological behavior. Since it's unlikely that even the most healthy of us can ever shed our needs for attention and approval completely, it's very important that we be able to honestly answer the question: "What do I do to get the attention of my fellow human beings, and am I going about getting my attention needs met in an open and healthy manner?" These are important questions because many of us are only marginally aware of our methods and motivations.

My son and I frequently talk about our attention needs and how we go about achieving them. Sometimes these discussions lead to the awareness that our current attempts to be recognized are not being conducted in a healthy manner.

People deal too much with
the negative, with what is
wrong...
Why not try and see
positive things, to just
touch those things and
make them bloom?

—*Tich Nhat Hanh*

11

The Most Wondrous Of Gifts

The greatest gift you can give your children is
the quality of your own life!

Sometimes when I recognize the importance of this fact, my mind reflects on all the times I've failed to model a high-quality life for my child. The result is guilt, grief, and sorrow. But instead of reflecting upon the missed opportunities, I force myself to recognize the overall picture. Even more importantly is the model I have the opportunity to be in the future. To know that the quality of my life is the greatest gift I can give, not just to my child but also to the world, should be a motivational kick in the pants and not cause for despair.

Let us sing a new song, not with our lips but with our lives.

—St. Augustine

<u>12</u>

Treat Your Children With Kindness

Point out to your children the simple fact that kind people are happy people, while unkind people are unhappy people. It doesn't take a Gallup Poll researcher to discover the worldwide validity of this obvious fact. Surprisingly, parents don't often think of treating their children with kindness. When is the last time you intentionally did something kind for your child? The vast majority of attention we give our children is scolding and trying to change their behavior in some way. Let's spend more time playing with them, appreciating them, and being actively kind. Let's spend less time judging them. If you praise children and treat them with respect and kindness, they'll grace the world with their kindness—and they'll bring happiness and joy to themselves and others. Kindness and high EQ are virtually synonymous.

. . . .

My religion is very simple: My religion is kindness.

—The Dalai Lama

. . . .

13

Cleaning Up Our Mistakes

Having a healthy EQ doesn't mean you go through life without making mistakes. Healthy EQ people are people who clean up the mistakes they do make. When you become aware that you've over-disciplined your children or have done something that didn't promote the development of their spirit, tell them what you did wrong, demonstrate to them how you should have handled it, and apologize to them. Many times during my tenure as a parent, I've apologized to my child, explained my faulty thinking, and made a verbal commitment to not behave that way in the future. If I violate my commitment, as I sometimes do, I make a verbal re-commitment and explain that even the best relationships sometimes involve conflict and discord. This affords all of us the opportunity to develop and discuss a healthy concept of forgiveness, mercy, and justice.

The outgrowth of this willingness to admit my shortcomings has been our son's willingness to express his regrets for his overreactions and unfairness. The expression "I'm sorry" is rampant within our household, and it is necessary to healthy human interactions everywhere. A sincere expression of "I'm sorry" is a grand opportunity for the experience of love and connection, which functions as an avenue for family unity.

❤❤❤❤❤❤❤❤❤❤❤❤❤❤❤❤❤❤❤❤❤❤❤❤❤❤❤❤❤❤❤❤

We spend so much time and energy judging others
that we don't have any left over for life.

—Father Rohr

<u>14</u>

Complete Your Relationship With Your Children On A Regular Basis

Completing your relationship means telling your children the things you would tell them if you knew that you, or they, had just twenty-four more hours to live. None of us has forever to live. Much of the pain that surrounds the death of a loved one involves the realization that we didn't get to say all the things we wanted to say to them. So say it to them now and do it regularly. Let your children know how much you love them and value their presence.

Do this with your spouse, parents, and friends as well. The expression of these feelings creates magical experiences with your family. On a number of occasions I've caught myself rushing out of the house in the morning on my way to work, shouting a good-bye that I hardly even meant. Suddenly I recognized that there was no guarantee that I'd be coming back, nor was there a guarantee that my wife and son would be there when and if I did come back. In these moments I go back in and express my love and appreciation. A marvelous way for us all to start the day is to tell our children and spouse what we would say if that was the last time we were ever to see them.

It's fine to plan to live forever—I encourage it— and also to live like each day was your last.

15

Convey The Importance Of The Moment To Your Children

All of the world's great religious traditions tell us that NOW is the only moment there really is and that each moment is for loving and forgiving. We must convey the importance of the moment to our children.

The poem that follows makes this point in a beautiful and sad way. It was written by a young woman and describes her relationship with her boyfriend. The poem was presented by Dr. Leo Buscaglia during a seminar at the University of Wisconsin entitled "What Is Essential Is Invisible to the Eye."

Remember the day I borrowed your brand new car and I dented it?
I thought you would kill me—but you didn't!
Remember the time I dragged you to the beach and you said it would rain and it did?
I thought you would say I told you so—but you didn't!
Do you remember the time that I flirted with all of the guys to make you jealous and you were?
I thought you would leave me—but you didn't!
And do you remember the time I spilled strawberry pie all over your car rug?
I thought you would hit me—but you didn't!
And remember the time I forgot to tell you that the dance was formal and you showed up in jeans?
I thought you would drop me—but you didn't!

Yes, there were lots of things you didn't do—but you put up with me, and you loved me, and you protected me—and there were lots of things that I wanted to make up to you when you returned from Vietnam—But you didn't.

—Anonymous

If there is any kindness I can show, or any good thing I can do to any fellow being, let me do it now, and not deter or neglect it, as I shall not pass this way again.

—William Penn

16

Speak From Your Heart, Not Your Head

There is a strong tendency to put what we say and do on automatic pilot. What was once an expression of true emotion becomes just a bunch of words. Even "I love you" becomes automatic and meaningless unless there's a conscious intention to deliver this message with true feeling from the heart. When you tell your children you love them, look them in the eyes. The eyes are the windows to the soul, and there is nothing richer than having a soul-to-soul contact with your children. Children who know they are truly loved and valued will have a healthy EQ.

> *Communication from anywhere other than the heart will never truly be heard. A message from the head is simply no match for a message from the heart.*

17

Make Love Primary, Standards Secondary

Don't let your relationship with your children become dominated by the struggle to have them meet the standards and expectations you have of them. Standards are fine, and some are necessary. Yet standards are secondary, while the love in the relationship is primary. Despite the fact that we say love is primary, it often becomes secondary and even nonexistent. The relationship then becomes about the standards.

If we had that same ten-hour video I mentioned at the beginning of this book, but of the last ten hours of interaction between you and your children, what would we see? Would we see a lot of loving interaction, or would we see a lot of conflict regarding standards? Standards such as pick up your clothes, finish your vegetables, do your homework now, or make your bed.

I want to stress again that standards are important, but standards are heavy anchors in the sea of parent-child relationships if they aren't delivered with love. I've found that it's quite difficult to get my child to do anything without being loving. Yet I can get him to do almost anything when I am loving. A household dominated by the struggle to implement standards has no love energy.

Love them, and leave them alone.

—Dr. Benjamin Spock

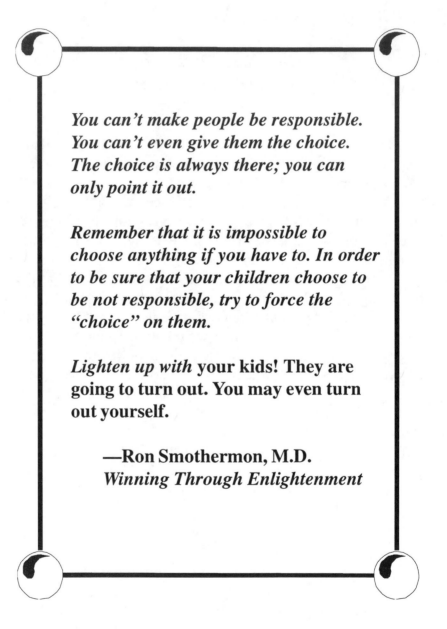

You can't make people be responsible. You can't even give them the choice. The choice is always there; you can only point it out.

Remember that it is impossible to choose anything if you have to. In order to be sure that your children choose to be not responsible, try to force the "choice" on them.

Lighten up with your kids! They are going to turn out. You may even turn out yourself.

—Ron Smothermon, M.D.
Winning Through Enlightenment

18

Give Your Children A Spiritual Basis From Which To Grow

Actively provide your children with a spiritual perspective. Many parents take pride in saying they're allowing their children to choose their own direction with regard to spirituality. But if your children don't get their spiritual outlook from you, who knows where it will come from or what they will get? Religious cults with their manipulative tactics are all too commonplace. It's important that our spiritual outlook be characterized by a lack of rigidity, an optimistic perspective, an appreciation for diversity, an acceptance and tolerance for non-group members, and a democratic set of governing principles with no hidden or secret agendas.

The following is a quote from Bo Lozoff, founder of the Human Kindness Foundation (Route 1, Box 201-N, Durham, NC 27705).

If a family doesn't provide a deep view about the purpose for being alive and the importance of respecting all beings, then our children will grow up lost, selfish, close-minded, angry, violent. Without lots of loving guidance from us, they meet a confusing and frightening world.

Obviously, it's important that we be clear about our purpose for being alive. All the major spiritual traditions boil down to a common theme: Have you unconditional love for yourself, for others, and for the creator of this mysterious Universe?

Let's look at the first requirement that is necessary in giving a child that longed-for meaning to live. We parents must possess a foundation upon which to base our lives and which can withstand the test of time. Something that will support us through every phase of living: adolescence, young adulthood, middle age, old age, marriage crises, financial crises, children's crises, energy crises, and especially a rapidly changing society in which spiritual values are swiftly eroding. We parents must have a crucial foundation upon which we base our lives in order to give it to our children. In my opinion, it is the most valuable treasure we can pass on to our offspring.

—Ross Campell, M.D.

19

Teach Your Children That "Having" Does Not Equal "Happy"

Let your children know that there is more to life than having everything that society sells. Having everything isn't nearly enough to give the lasting experience of joy and aliveness. To go beyond our words, we must model a life that isn't oriented toward the constant pursuit of bigger and better things. The natural desire we all have for possessions we think will make us happy forever is greatly compounded in our society by the science of advertising. So it is essential that we not be taken in by the myth of the American Dream. The person who dies with the most toys does not win. It's vitally important that we clearly distinguish between our experiences and our beliefs and that we teach our children to do the same. Just how much lasting happiness did our last new purchase provide us? Is the pride of home ownership anything more than a bunch of words? Yet the belief is that if we can acquire the right things, the quality of our life will change. The experience is that the quality of our life doesn't change very much when we acquire all the items that make up the American Dream. Just how happy are all the people who already possess all the things we want to possess? Even when our children are young, it's not too early to pose these types of questions. It will lay the foundation for them to ask themselves these very same questions later in life.

We must let our children recognize that there is a great confusion between quantity and quality in our society. Quantity in our life doesn't lead to quality in our life. There is a vast difference between a life dedicated to meeting our needs and a life dedicated to meeting our wants. Meeting our needs is fairly simple in our society. Meeting all our wants is simply impossible. Let your children know the difference between "wants" and "needs" and help them make the distinction.

In much of the rest of the world, people have difficulty meeting their basic needs for food, water, shelter, and love. Helping other people meet their basic needs is a marvelous way to experience the joy and satisfaction we are all looking for. Kind people are happy people.

Let us focus on loving individuals and using objects,
rather than loving objects and using individuals.

*To receive everything,
one must open
one's hands
and give.*

—Taisen Deshimara

*So much of life, in today's world, has to do with **getting**. Values, in contrast, have to do with **being** and with **giving**. It is who we are and what we give rather than what we have that makes up our truest inner selves.*

—Linda and Richard Eyre
Teaching Your Children Values

<u>20</u>

Teach Your Children That There Is A Difference Between Pleasure And Happiness

We confuse pleasure and happiness in our society. Pleasure is short-term. It's the result of going out and getting something the external world has to offer. We can go to a good movie, buy a nice dinner, or buy our children or ourselves a new toy. The nature of pleasure is that it ends and is relatively brief. The positive sensations associated with a good meal don't last very long, and they actually become negative if we eat too much. All pleasurable experiences become negative if we continue to indulge without restraint. The use of drugs is the ultimate pleasure and the ultimate disaster. Happiness, on the other hand, is not so much something we go out and get, as it is a place we come from. We can't go out and get happiness, but we can *be* happy. One of the greatest gifts we can give to our children is our own happiness and cheerfulness, and the demonstration that these qualities are not bound to the constant pursuit of pleasure.

One of the fruitless things we often do in our culture is to try to quickly go from one pleasure to the next, hoping that if we can avoid any gaps between our pleasures the mosaic that we jam together will be one that affords us the constant sensation of "being happy." So we get up in the morning, have a delicious breakfast, play eighteen holes of golf, have a delicious lunch, shop for a new car, buy some clothes, have a delicious supper, buy an expensive wine, rent a video, buy snacks to eat during the video, have sex after the video, and go to bed on an expensive mattress that guarantees eight hours of pleasurable sleep. Understand, there's nothing wrong with this scenario—it just doesn't have much to do with happiness.

21

Let Your Children Know That Everyone Has An "Inner Critic"

Don't contribute to your child's "inner critic." The inner critic is that voice in our mind that tells us all sorts of negative things that are not true. Early on in life we start criticizing ourselves because we internalize the voices of our parents, friends, and society. We look in the mirror and call ourselves short, fat, ugly, plain, unacceptable, unlikeable, unloveable, stupid, hopeless, untalented, friendless, and on and on. The problem with the inner critic is that when its voice is telling us all these things, we actually believe every word and therefore feel hopeless, unloveable, stupid, etc. When we encourage our children to express their thoughts and feelings to us, we can become aware of the way in which they criticize themselves and then assist them to challenge these irrational, untrue inner thoughts. Not a single human being on the face of the planet is going to avoid having a big, mean, and ugly inner critic. Our task as parents is to help our children become aware of this monster and to get them to recognize that if they aren't feeling good, the inner critic is probably telling them some lie about themselves. Of course, it is vitally necessary for parents to develop the "awareness center," which is the foe of the inner critic. The "awareness center" is the positive self-image that tells us we are loveable, useful, acceptable, valuable, talented, beautiful, and smart. As parents, it is necessary to plant that voice in our children's minds early on in life, and to never stop nourishing and watering these flower-like qualities at every opportunity.

The open mind and the open heart hold no secrets—
only I love you.
                                        —K. Bradford Brown

It is something to be able to paint a particular picture, or to carve a statue, and so to make a few objects beautiful; but it is far more glorious to carve and paint the very atmosphere and medium through which we look. To affect the quality of the day—that is the highest of arts.

—Henry David Thoreau

22

Teach Your Children The Difference Between Guilt And Conscience

As parents we must distinguish for ourselves, and help our children distinguish, between the inner critic, conscience, guilt, and self-forgiveness. Many people, psychologists included, believe guilt is a useful emotion. They believe that guilty feelings about doing something that violates societal standards will inhibit the performance of the act, *and* they believe that feeling guilty after doing something that violates certain internal or external standards will keep us from doing the same thing again. This whole idea is well accepted primarily because we can't think of any other reason why people just wouldn't run wild and do anything they wanted to do. I would like to take a stand and say that guilt, which is part of our inner critic, is useless. Not only does it make us feel bad, it actually paves the way for the continuation of the behavior about which we feel guilty. The revolutionary idea that feeling guilty about something actually ensures that the same thing will be done again comes from an author I've previously mentioned, Ron Smothermon, M.D. In W*inning Through Enlightenment,* Smothermon states, "Guilt is the currency used to repay some real or imagined trespass so that the trespass can be repeated. Guilt therefore is an integral part of a cycle: trespass-guilt-trespass-guilt-trespass-guilt-trespass-guilt... and on and on forever. Guilt has absolutely no function in stopping something that is harmful. If you stop in a condition of guilt, it is despite the guilt, not because of it."

This idea is so revolutionary that it will likely be met with strong resistance. I strongly resisted this concept myself until I examined the usefulness of my own experiences of guilt. Sure enough, the things I felt guilty about were the things I repeated. After fifty-three years of living with and experiencing my own guilt-repeat-guilt-repeat cycle, combined with twenty years of full-time work with inmates as a prison psychologist in three United States penitentiaries, you would think that I would have noticed this obvious point: guilt not only doesn't decrease our negative behaviors, it guarantees their repetition.

If guilt isn't the answer, what is? One of the things we can do for our children, and ourselves, is to reduce the number of things we feel guilty about. The general rule in our household is: If your behavior doesn't physically or emotionally hurt someone else, and it doesn't physically hurt you, it's probably O.K. to do.

Don't promote guilt in your children. Actively try to eliminate guilt when you find it. People don't need guilt to behave properly; they need awareness. Awareness of what? Awareness that behaving a certain way has built-in intrinsic rewards and that behaving in other ways has built-in negative consequences. Awareness that some actions increase our separateness and pain, while other actions contribute to our natural joy and connection with other beings. Once we become aware that we are all in this thing called *Life* together, it becomes increasingly difficult to behave in ways that result in harm to others or ourselves. We must come to the point of being aware that harming others is really a form of self-harm. Therefore, teach your children the awareness of the universal principles and avoid breeding guilt.

The <u>Law of Gravity</u> is a universal principal. If you jump off a three-story building you will pay the consequences. We need to recognize what might be called the <u>Law of Hatred</u>, because if you hate, you will pay the consequences .

23

We Must Be Self-Forgiving And Forgiveness-Seeking

As human beings, we will all make mistakes that will hurt other people. Let's give up guilt, ask for forgiveness from those we've hurt, say we're sorry, and forgive ourselves for what was done. That is what we need to encourage our children to do. The best encouragement for them is to hear us ask their forgiveness after we've treated them unfairly, and to see that we can forgive ourselves as we commit to not being unfair in the future. This practice has brought great peace and joy into our household. Asking forgiveness brings a family closer and closer together.

Every choice to blame others,
to believe we are guilty when they blame us,
or to blame ourselves, is an act of violence to our own soul.

—Nancy H. Glende

Our ability to forgive can save us all. If only I could
forgive and forget as swiftly and completely as my
trusted family dog!

24

Teach Your Children That The Universe Is A Safe Place

Albert Einstein is most commonly known for his intellectual genius. But Einstein was also a compassionate and caring man who was deeply spiritual and concerned with the conditions of his world. He was a person of both very high IQ and very high EQ. Einstein believed, and made a statement to the effect, that the most important thing you can know about someone is whether or not hc views the Universe as a safe place. This is a vitally important question for us all to answer because it is in essence the backdrop against which we view everything else. Clearly, there are very strong EQ implications for the way in which people view the world they live in. Criminals, juvenile delinquents, and psychologically unhealthy people—people with low EQ—all view the world as a dangerous place.

People who view the world as such have collected a great deal of evidence to support their perspective. Reading the newspaper and watching the six o'clock news can provide plenty of support for the "dangerous world" viewpoint. But the six o'clock news is a lie. It presents just one small portion of the pie and then implies that it represents the entire pie. After watching television news broadcasts and reading front-page newspaper coverage, it would be easy to assume that the vast majority of deaths in the world are the result of murder, mayhem, and bizarre behavior. To be sure, these circumstances do happen, but they're just a slice of the bigger pie. Peaceful deaths involving no unusual circumstances simply do not make the news report.

People having the view that the Universe is basically a safe place have also collected a lot of evidence to support their core belief. At one level, I don't know whether the Universe is a safe place or not, although I *believe* it is. What I do know is that every human being has already made that decision whether they are aware of it or not. And what I also know is that people who view the world as a basically safe place are healthier, happier, and enjoy a higher EQ than those who don't. I also know that people who view the world dangerously are much more likely to be dangerous and to contribute to the danger that does exist. At a subtle psychological level, we are all bent on proving to ourselves and others that our world view is accurate. Consequently, birds of a feather do flock together because it affords the opportunity to reinforce the existing position. I surmise that changing a person's world view is much more difficult than establishing one. From this perspective, teach your children that the Universe is a safe place. It is one of the nicest gifts you can provide to them—and to the rest of the world.

If you view the Universe as a dangerous place, you will draw violence into your life, you will be <u>against</u> other people, and your life will be about survival. If you view the Universe as a safe place, you will draw harmony into your life, you will be <u>for</u> other people, and your life will be about contribution.

25

Teach Learned Optimism And Beware Of Learned Helplessness

Years ago, Dr. Martin Seligman conducted research with animals that involved electric shock the animals could not avoid in any way. Eventually these animals became listless and appeared to simply resign themselves to their fate. A second part of the experiment afforded these animals an opportunity to learn a simple response that would allow them the opportunity to escape from the shock. Many of these animals did not even attempt to learn the escape response, but instead simply gave up and continued to receive the shock. Research with humans (not involving shock) tended to produce similar findings. These findings are referred to as learned helplessness. Literally, animals and people can learn to be helpless by being continually exposed to unavoidable aversive situations and events. With humans, helplessness seems to occur when we come to believe that events are not within our control. Children appear most vulnerable to being in unavoidable positions. Physical or verbal abuse is not something they can avoid very easily. Thus, abused children develop the cognitive mindset that they are helpless, and this core belief is reflected in every area of their life, even in situations in which they clearly are not helpless. The tendency to give up is closely related to depression, anxiety, and low self-esteem.

It's important to recognize, however, that even the most loving parents may unknowingly create situations that encourage feelings of helplessness. When we expect perfection and repeatedly diminish our children's accomplishments, we're making a statement that they can never do enough to matter. On the other hand, when we protect our children from the consequences of their behavior by smoothing over their every mistake, we're gradually creating a mindset that what they do doesn't make a difference at all. The most important thing a parent can do is to assist the child in recognizing mistakes and putting them in their proper context. Most mistakes are not the end of the world and can be corrected.

Whatever the case, it's extremely important that we not create situations whereby our children come to believe in the futility of their actions. Once the mindset of learned helplessness is established it's difficult (but not impossible) to correct. Clearly, prevention is easier than cure. But we can do even better than mere prevention. We can actively promote optimism. Once again, it's the model that we as parents present to our children that really counts. Research indicates that children tend to explain life in the same way their mother explains it. Consequently, the child's level of optimism is very similar to the parents' level of optimism. For a thorough review of this entire subject, see the excellent book called *Learned Optimism* by Martin E. P. Seligman, Ph.D.

Shoot for the moon. Even if you miss it you will land among the stars.

—Les Brown

<u>26</u>

Our Enemy Is The Position Of Helplessness

Don't let your children become the "enemy," and teach them who the "enemy" is in our society. Norman Cousins uses the term "enemy" in his book *Human Options: An Autobiographical Notebook*. While he offers a number of examples of who the enemy is in our culture, the following quotation from his book is particularly relevant to our current discussion. Cousins states:

> *"The enemy is a man who not only believes in his own helplessness but actually worships it. His main article of faith is that there are mammoth forces at work that the individual cannot possibly comprehend, much less alter or direct. And so he expends vast energies in attempting to convince other people that there is nothing they can do. He is the enemy because of the proximity of helplessness to hopelessness."*

In each of us lies a space in which this enemy dwells. High EQ people have brought the enemy out of the darkness and into the light, where they can control its influence and not pass the enemy from their minds to the minds of their children and others.

Let your children know that they are the captains of their ship and they can choose to be peaceful no matter what the external world presents to them at the time.

The secret of life is to have a task, something you devote your entire life to, something you bring everything to, every minute of the day for the rest of your life. And the most important thing, it must be something you cannot possibly do.

—Henry Moore

This world is a test tube in the experiment of life, perhaps the only one. It may still be that one of the creatures in this test tube will destroy the test tube. The outcome cannot be known, and exists in a state of uncertainty. Your actions and your thoughts right now are part of the process which determines the outcome of the experiment. The choice to be loyal to all beings is the choice for the experiment to work. The choice to be disloyal, even in small ways is a vote to blow away the experiment of life.

—Ron Smothermon, M.D.

*Handbook For The Third Millennium:
2000 and Beyond*

27

Model A Life Of Service And Find Happiness

Albert Schweitzer made the statement, "I don't know what your destiny will be, but one thing I do know: the only ones among you who will be happy are those who have sought and found how to serve."

As parents, we don't know what the specific destinies of our children will be. The goal of every healthy parent is to have decent, happy, spiritually responsible children who make a positive contribution to our world. To help them attain this goal we must assist them in finding their own avenue of service to others. What better way to assist them than by modeling a life that involves service, and by pointing out to them that the happiest are those who made the most people happy—and the saddest are those who made the most people sad. Creating happy children is the most fundamental and important service you can do for the world.

We are each of us angels with only one wing.
And we can only fly embracing each other.

—Luciano De Crescenzo

Let us not be satisfied with giving money. Money is not enough, money can be got, but they need your hearts to love them. So spread your love everywhere you go—first of all in your own home. Give love to your children, to your wife or husband, to the next-door neighbor.

—Mother Teresa

<u>28</u>

Your Children Are Here For The Benefit Of Humankind's Sake

Life is not about getting, getting, getting...
It's about giving, giving, giving!

Many of the world's religious traditions agree that there is "a spirit within us that delights in doing no evil!" Let us nourish, acknowledge, and awaken that spirit in every way we possibly can in our children. One of the ways I do this is to send poems to my son on special occasions throughout the year. He always looks beyond my clumsy attempts to be poetic and gets the deeper message that we are all here to serve and be served. The following is the last few lines of a lengthy poem I presented to my son on his eighteenth birthday:

It's not about possessions or being attractive or smart
I'm speaking of things that relate to the heart
It's not because I'm your dad that I think this way
So trust me, my son, I know what I say
Your presence on Earth is not a mistake
You are here for the benefit of Humankind's sake.

Whether it's through poetry or some other heart-felt expression, let your children know that it is their basic goodness and not appearances that counts.

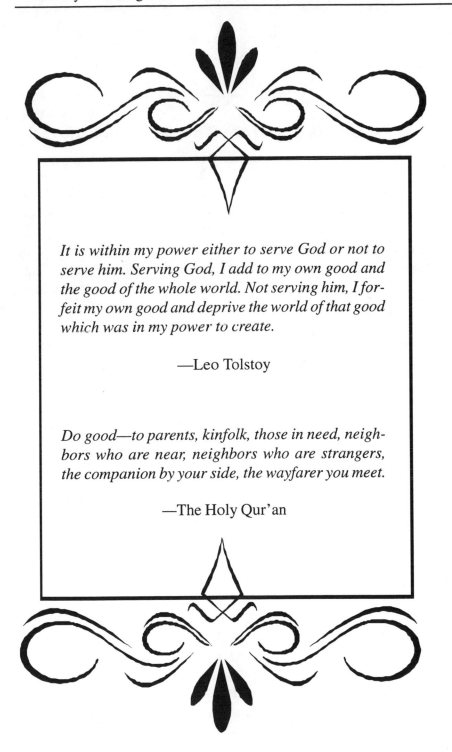

It is within my power either to serve God or not to serve him. Serving God, I add to my own good and the good of the whole world. Not serving him, I forfeit my own good and deprive the world of that good which was in my power to create.

—Leo Tolstoy

Do good—to parents, kinfolk, those in need, neighbors who are near, neighbors who are strangers, the companion by your side, the wayfarer you meet.

—The Holy Qur'an

29

Life Is A Journey That Is To Be Enjoyed

The inability to delay gratification is a well-recognized sign of a low EQ. But there is a not very well recognized trap that responsible people can fall into when they engage in the traditional delay of gratification model. At some level, the traditional model is "bite the bullet now and you'll be happy later." Biting the bullet isn't fun—it's what you have to do to have fun later. Going to college is the classic example. If you bite the bullet for four years, you'll have fun for the next fifty. But this model ignores our experience. It ignores the sage realization that there are two great disappointments in life. One is to set a goal and not achieve it, while the second is to set a goal *and* achieve it. To be sure, there's a brief period of satisfaction when we attain our goals, but the nature of things doesn't allow for us to bask in this glory too long—we must move on. And if we didn't enjoy the taste of the bullet, it becomes increasingly more difficult to set goals, due to the growing awareness that achieving them doesn't quite get us to where we'd expected to be. The alternative to this traditional model may be best conveyed by telling this short story:

A monk was peacefully attending to his worldly duties when he heard a loud thundering growl in the distance. He looked in the direction of the sound and saw that there was a very hungry-looking tiger running toward him. The monk began to run away, yet he could clearly hear that the tiger was gaining ground. After some moments of running, the monk came to a huge cliff with a drop of more than a hundred feet. He looked back and saw that the tiger was only a short distance away. He looked down and decided to jump. Just as he jumped, he noticed a wild strawberry vine on the edge of the cliff. On the vine was the biggest ripe strawberry he had ever seen. He quickly snatched the strawberry in mid-air and ate it as he tumbled to his death.

This monk was enjoying the trip; he was reaching for all the gusto he could while he had the chance.

We must teach our children that life is a process, not so much a destination as a trip, and it is the trip that must be enjoyed. The trip is not about biting the bullet, it's about biting the strawberry. Much of the drug abuse and alcoholism in otherwise basically responsible middle-class Americans is the result of the awareness that all this delay of gratification hasn't been very much fun; and, to make things worse, there hasn't been much gratification at the end either.

The traditional idea of success, which portrays life to be like a mountain that must be climbed dutifully and with great effort all the way to the top, is not the way it works—because the mountain of life has no top. There is no place to get to where we can kick back forever and be blissfully happy. We can, however, enjoy the trip up the mountain just like the monk in our story.

Let your child know that life is a journey that is to be enjoyed. If you enjoy your trip, they will enjoy theirs.

Follow your bliss, but recognize that the bliss is found more in the trip than in the destination.

30

Listen To Your Children

A lot of emphasis is being placed on effective communication skills these days. Most of us think this means learning to talk more effectively. Rarely does someone say, "I need to learn how to listen." We think that since we have two ears we obviously listen well. We don't think that listening is a skill requiring tremendous effort. In *The Road Less Traveled* by M. Scott Peck, the author tells us that listening is an act of love and that our willingness to listen to our children is the best possible concrete evidence we can provide to them that we do love them. Dr. Peck's entire book is on the "must" reading list for anyone interested in EQ development. Listen to your children. They'll know that you love them and they'll listen to you for the same reason you listen to them—because of love.

The heart of a fool is in his mouth,
but the mouth of a wise man is in his heart.

—Benjamin Franklin

<u>31</u>

Allow Your Children The Experience Of Power

People who truly *feel* powerful are not power-hungry. Much of the evil that exists in the world is the result of a deep sense of powerlessness. Don't give your children the feeling that they're powerless. There are essentially three approaches to child-rearing. In the authoritarian approach, power within the family is confined to the parents—most generally an overly strict and dominant father figure. Rigid rules, physical punishment, and verbal harassment characterize the interactions within the authoritarian household. The dominant parent(s) is like a military sergeant and the children are like new recruits in basic training. Children are to be seen and not heard, and they don't have a voice in the decision-making processes that go on within the family. With the authoritarian child-rearing strategy, children are likely to develop a strong sense of powerlessness.

The second type of child-rearing environment is laissez faire. In a laissez faire atmosphere there are no rules, and the children are more or less left to fend for themselves. The parents in this situation are generally too overly burdened with physical, psychological, socioeconomic, or drug abuse problems to pay loving attention or provide an appropriate rule structure to the children. The children in this situation are also unlikely to develop a healthy sense of power.

The third child-rearing strategy is democratic in nature. In families in which this strategy is used, the child's opinion is valued. Family decisions resemble a democratic process in which everyone's vote within the family is given full consideration. For example, if there's a choice between going for a drive into town or going to a movie, the children are invited into the decision-making process. Thus, they acquire the belief that who they are counts, and what they say and do really matters. They feel empowered, not powerless.

Truly powerful people are big enough to give their power away. Anything you hoard has you, rather than you having it. You cannot truly have anything you cannot freely give away. This is especially true with power.

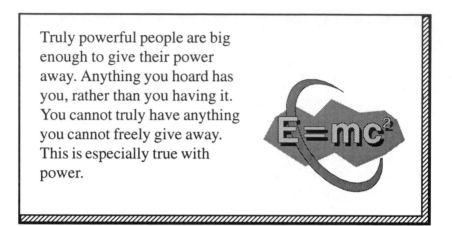

<u>32</u>

Help Your Children Become Internally Oriented And Not Externally Oriented

Psychologists like to divide people up into categories. Tests can evaluate whether people believe that external circumstances—forces outside of themselves—control their behavior and feelings, or whether factors inside themselves determine their emotions and actions. This whole area of study is called attribution theory. Attribution theory asks, "What factors do people attribute *their* behavior to? What factors do they attribute the behavior of other people to? How do they explain what happens to them—do they use internal or external explanations? Are they responsible for their behavior or are external forces responsible?"

This field of study has yielded some truly fascinating information. First of all, studies indicate that when we explain our *own* behavior we generally do so by citing external causes. For example, when we explain our anger to someone else, we're likely to blame someone other than ourselves—things external to us. Yet when we explain the behavior of *other* people, we most often use explanations that are *internal* to them. I get angry at you because you're an inconsiderate jerk. You get angry at me because you're selfish, close-minded, and violent. I don't get angry because I'm selfish, close-minded, and violent. So it is that I account for my anger because of you (external reasons) and explain your anger because of you (internal reasons).

The issue is one of responsibility. Who really causes what? To be sure, there are external events in our lives, but each of us makes something unique out of the events the Universe presents to us. Is my electric bill a source of frustration and anger, or am I focusing on how fortunate I am to have a source of power that much of the rest of world lacks?

As parents, we need to promote our children's internal orientation and discourage anything that promotes the idea that we are poor victims of life. The language we use to explain our behavior in the presence of our children is crucial to their development. When a parent shouts "You make me so mad when you do that!", he is passing on an external view of the world that says "I feel the way I do because of you." When we as parents make mistakes in this area (and we will all make many of them), it's important to talk to our children and clear up the mistake. Let them know that you lost sight of the fact that you have a choice. Let them know who really does it to us, because it is we ourselves. Give them the gift of being responsible for their feelings and behavior. Let them know that taking responsibility for their lives is the second most difficult thing in the world to do. The only thing more difficult is to be a victim of external events. Let your children know they can choose to be happy inside, regardless of what is happening outside.

What life means to us is determined not so much by what life brings to us as by the attitude we bring to life; not so much by what happens to us as by our reaction to what happens.

—Lewis L. Dunnington

33

Don't Go To Bed At Night Without Telling Your Children You Love Them

Hopefully, even low EQ parents tuck their young children into bed at night. As our children get older, the likelihood of negative interaction increases, then suddenly one night we go to bed angry and fail to say goodnight to them. If this is done two or three times, it becomes a pattern. Don't let this happen. Even if you're angry, don't fail to let your children know that your love transcends your anger. It's perfectly O.K. to say, "I'm angry right now *and* I love you." We're showing our children that we are bigger than our emotions, and they'll know that they are bigger than theirs. Anger and negativity will grow and fester overnight, even as we sleep, and we'll awaken in the morning with a heavy heart and heavy thoughts. Make the commitment to never go to bed without acknowledging your children. The reward is a psychologically healthy teenager who will sheepishly ask for a hug at night. Suddenly, you will know in your heart that parenting is all worthwhile.

The only thing I know that truly heals people is unconditional love.

—Elizabeth Kűbler-Ross

34

We Have A Choice Between
Peace And Conflict, Between Love And Fear

One of the guidelines promoted by the numerous Attitudinal Healing Centers that exist throughout the world is "We agree to keep in mind that we always have a choice between peace and conflict, between love and fear." Always make your children aware of that choice. As parents, we must remain aware of it ourselves. Awareness is the key word here because who, in his right mind, would ever choose conflict over peace? Every time we argue with our spouse or our children, we're choosing conflict and hatred over love and harmony. We actually only engage in conflict rather than peace when we aren't sufficiently aware to make the sensible choice. Teach your children to be aware, to make the choice of peace over conflict, and of love over fear.

Actually, awareness does not bring us back to our "right" mind—it puts us back in touch with our heart, which is always right."

35

When Making Choices, Choose The Option Involving The Greater Degree Of Love

Let your children know that they'll be faced with many choices during their lifetime. Teach them that there are basically two types of choice situations. One type of situation involves choices that don't involve love. The choice you make in this type of situation is really not very important to your life, even though it may feel that way at the time. No one lies on his deathbed wishing he would have bought the green car instead of the red, worn the pearl earrings instead of the diamonds, or purchased plush carpet instead of the short fiber. When faced with a choice situation that doesn't involve love, just make the choice and get on with your life.

The second type of choice situation involves love. The guideline here is simple: choose in the direction of the most love. Decisions in this arena of choice are important. People do lie on their deathbeds wishing they had made up with their sister, father, or mother. Always choose in the direction of love. These choices pay immediate as well as long-term dividends.

It is only with the heart that one sees rightly,
what is essential is invisible to the eye.

—Antoine de Saint-Exupery,
The Little Prince

36

Help Your Children Distinguish Between Ego-Esteem And Self-Esteem

Ego-esteem is the praise we get from others that makes us feel good. There's nothing wrong with ego-esteem; it's just that it's impossible to get enough of it to really convince someone who doesn't have self-esteem that he's really O.K. Ego-esteem comes from the outside—it's when someone else tells us we're fantastic. Self-esteem comes from the inside. It's when we tell ourselves we're fantastic.

Without a good healthy level of self-esteem one has the constant need for outside validation to achieve a sense of self-worth, and it's never enough. Many juvenile delinquents have low self-esteem and are therefore in constant need of external praise, which can easily be provided by gang membership. Teach your children to monitor what they internally say to themselves about themselves. If they don't think they're special, nobody else can convince them of it. We are ultimately special because we say so, not because someone else says so.

Children *learn* to have low self-esteem. As parents, it's important for us not to rob them of the naturally high regard they have for themselves when they enter the world.

And let us not forget that the level of regard we hold for our fellow creatures is remarkably similar to the level of regard we have for ourselves.

<u>37</u>

Let Your Children Know That We Are All In This Thing Called Life Together

Either we are all going to make it or none of us is going to make it. Someone once said that on this spaceship called Earth, there are no passengers, just working crew members.

In the previously cited book *Human Options: An Autobiographical Notebook* by Norman Cousins, the author writes, "The enemy is many people. He is the man whose only concern about the world is that it stays in one piece during his own lifetime." Later Cousins states, "Nothing to him is less important than the shape of things to come or the needs of the next generation." Finally, Cousins tells us, "When he thinks about the world at all, it is usually in terms of his hope that the atomic fireworks can be postponed for fifteen or twenty years. He is the enemy because nothing less than a passionate concern for the rights of unborn legions will enable the world itself to become connected and whole."

Teach your children this passionate concern by demonstrating it yourself.

Those who do good as opportunity offers are sowing seeds all the time and they need not doubt the harvest.

—George Bernard Shaw

38

Teach Your Children To Focus On The Big Picture

Let your children know that when it comes to problems in life, they have two options. They can focus on their own petty problems and become totally consumed with them, or they can focus on the big picture, on the problems of the world, and deal with them. The trap is to believe that we'll help with the big picture once we solve our own problems. We never get that far. The reality is that when we work on the world's big problems, our own seem smaller.

The sense of making a difference in life is a natural condition with children. Young children don't need alarm clocks to wake them up. They wake up because they crave the sense of aliveness offered by a day full of opportunities to make a difference. Children naturally view themselves as contributors. The harshness of parenting and a negative environment can turn them into survivors. Jesus tells us that unless we become little children again we cannot enter into the Kingdom of Heaven. Change the framework of your life by becoming a contributor instead of a struggling survivor.

Helen Keller asked the question, "Do you get up in the morning because the alarm clock rings, or do you get up because it makes a difference?" When we focus exclusively on our own petty issues, there's no sense of meaning or aliveness in our life—we need an alarm clock to wake us up. When we have a purpose beyond ourselves, when we focus on being a contributor to solving some of the world's problems, we wake up in the morning alive and with the awareness that we make a difference—no alarm clock needed.

Don't be confused—the problems we have in life don't go away. We'll still get flat tires, bills will have to be paid, and refrigerators will need repair. But these aggravations move from center stage and become secondary, while the contributions we make to life become primary.

High EQ people view themselves as contributors, while low EQ's are survivors. Contributors survive too, and with so much more joy and ease than do survivors. Haven't you noticed?

See Everything.
Overlook a great deal.
Improve a little.

—Pope John XXIII

Far and away
the best prize that life offers
is the chance to work hard
at work worth doing.

—Theodore Roosevelt

39

TeachYour Children That They Make A Difference In OurWorld

Don't let the following story become a reality in the life of your children:

In the beginning, the Universe was yours and it was all perfect. You felt like you were this magnificent bubble floating through space. You experienced total peace and harmony in your bubble. On your bubble, clearly printed for all the Universe to see, was inscribed, "I make a difference, it matters that I live." As you moved through this marvelous Universe where everything you did was a daring adventure, you noticed, barely noticed, a small speck of an object that looked to be so far away that it appeared to be in the distant corner of another universe. A year later you looked over your shoulder and noticed that this small speck was slightly larger and now appeared to be contained within your own Universe. You hardly noticed and went back to making a difference in life. Another year or so later, you noticed that this object was now quite large and was definitely contained within the confines of your Universe. You chose not to pay much attention and went back to making a difference in a world full of adventure and excitement.

Over the course of the next several years you paid an increasing amount of attention to this object and noticed that it was getting closer and closer, faster and faster.

Now you can see that it is a box that is approaching—and you notice in the distance that this box has written on it, "You don't make a difference!" A few days later you look up and see that your bubble, which on the outside reads, "I make a difference," is face to face with the box which reads, "You don't make a difference." Suddenly, you hear a loud popping sound, as if a balloon has just burst, and when you look around you see that the "You don't make a difference" box is gone. You feel somewhat relieved, but somehow you don't feel the same. Something is wrong, but you don't know what it is. You don't feel much aliveness anymore and you now need an alarm clock to get up in the morning. Things inside your bubble are now heavy and negative, and your bubble now seems to have walls. Anyway, you keep floating around in the Universe—floating around in a box that clearly states on each of the six outside walls, "You don't make a difference."

Unfortunately, some degree of this scenario will very likely touch the life of every child. But all is not lost, because there is something else written on the outside of the box in addition to the words "You don't make a difference." The instructions for how to escape from the box are also clearly stated. Of course, someone inside the box can't read the instructions for getting out. As parents, your job is to read the instructions to your children over and over and over again. If you're a parent on the inside of the box, listen carefully for the words that are coming from the outside, for they may be the instructions for your escape. It may even be your own child who is reading you these instructions. Listen carefully! You do make a difference!

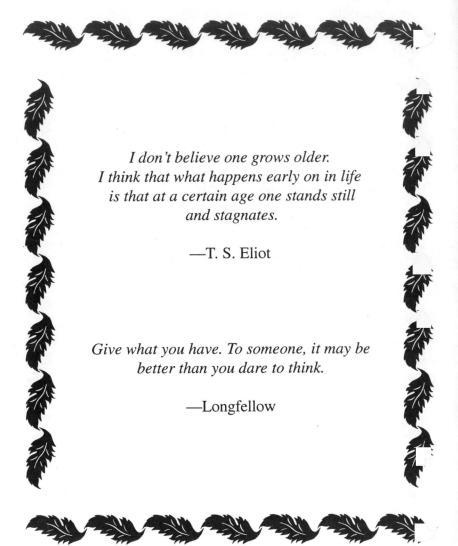

I don't believe one grows older.
I think that what happens early on in life
is that at a certain age one stands still
and stagnates.

—T. S. Eliot

Give what you have. To someone, it may be
better than you dare to think.

—Longfellow

40

Assume The Role Of A Contributor To Your Children And To The World

Whatever it is you do with your children, make sure it is a contribution to them. Don't assume that you'll work at other things in your life now so that you'll be better able to contribute to them later. They want and need your love now.

Remember that kind people are happy people, and what we want most for our children is that they be happy. Contribute to your children and they will contribute to you and the world, and they will be happy.

Give the best that you have and the highest you know—and do it now.

—Ralph W. Sockman

41

Let Your Children Know That The Universe Has A Grain To It

When one goes against the grain of the Universe, life is rough. The Universe is designed to get your attention when you're going against its laws—its grain. The Universe obviously has physical laws. If you fall from a ten-foot roof, the ground will get your attention. The Universe also has metaphysical laws. The Russian sage, Gurdjieff, informed us, "If you help others, you will be helped, perhaps tomorrow, perhaps in one hundred years, but you will be helped. Nature must pay off the debt." Helping others is going with the flow; hindering others is going against the grain. A life of selfishness is punishment enough—and it might even be worse.

As a person resists noticing the Universe's early attempts to provide wake-up calls, life's lessons become progressively harsher. Depression, anxiety, divorce, prison, drug addiction, more prison—all these are attempts to let us know we've taken the wrong path. Eventually, life will become one tragedy after another. Tragedy and struggle characterize the life of low EQ people.

So, walk the right path. Walk it hand in hand with your children, and always let your life speak louder than your words. The consequences will be peace, harmony, aliveness, loving relationships, and connectedness.

Some of us jump into the stream of life and try to
swim upstream, wondering the whole time why
Life is so tough and tiresome.

42

The Enemy Is Within, Not Without

The most important battles your children will have to fight are those that are waged between their own two ears. Throughout their entire life they will have to do battle with the emotions and thoughts of prejudice, anger, doubt, fear, desire, laziness, sorrow, boredom, and others. Prepare them for these battles. Encourage them to share their feelings, thoughts, troubles, and problems. That which we talk about becomes smaller, somehow more manageable. Support groups of every possible variety exist in most large communities. They offer the opportunity to be served and to be of service. Let your children see that you're courageous enough to attend these growth-oriented activities. They'll naturally follow in this same direction when they experience the need for their own growth and support.

I have only three enemies. My favorite enemy, the one most easily influenced for the better, is the British Empire. My second enemy, the Indian people, is far more difficult. But my most formidable opponent is a man named Mohandas K. Gandhi. With him I seem to have very little influence

—Mohandas K. Gandhi

43

Become A Responsible Friend To Your Children

Let your children know you are their friend, and let them know what it means to be a friend. The following is a poem my wife wrote to our son on his thirteenth birthday.

I WAS THERE

I was there when he was born
Saw the fear within his eyes
I picked him up, I held him close
And gently soothed his cries.

I was there when he was just past one
He took that careful step
I applauded him, I got his Dad
We laughed so hard we wept.

I was there when he was five
To school I sent him packin'
With paper, glue, and crayon stix
His lunch box nothing lackin'.

I was there when he was twelve
When death first pierced his heart
In his pain I saw myself
The child-like tender part.

He's thirteen now, and I'm still there
His face almost a man's
I watch him as he talks with girls,
I watch as they hold hands.

But my job, I know, is far from done
There'll be broken hearts to mend
I'll be there cause I'm his Mom
But most of all cause I'm his friend.

True friendship is difficult to define. I've talked with some low EQ parents who boasted about having a close friendship with their children. They talked about drinking alcohol and smoking marijuana together and letting their children "do their own thing." This is the type of friendship their children can get from gang members.

A very close friend of ours once told us how she quit using marijuana. She was in her twenties and was talking to the young son of some close friends. Boasting, she was telling the child how lucky he was to have parents who were so "hip" that they smoked marijuana openly and lived without society's usual constraints. The child looked up at her and said, "What? How can you say I'm lucky? Mom and Dad barely know I'm here—all I do is listen to you guys laugh about dumb things!"

Our friend quit using marijuana that day. I suspect the child's parents did the same. Unfortunately, many parents persist in this kind of behavior. Somehow they continue with the illusion that they are "good buddies" with their children—which I believe only serves the purpose of allowing them to behave like children, while their children are thrown into the lonely role of fending for themselves.

The type of friendship I speak of involves the promise to support your children to live by the standards to which you are mutually committed. It involves the understanding that you are partners in life and that any failure to support them to live a life of high standards is really support for them to live by low standards.

You are both 100 percent responsible for your own behavior and 100 percent responsible for their behavior. That's a total of 200 percent responsibility, and that should be sufficient to carry us through.

A friend is one to whom one may pour out all the contents of one's heart, chaff and grain together, knowing that the gentlest of hands will take and sift it, keep what is worth keeping and with a breath of kindness blow the rest away.

—Arabian Proverb

44

Trust That Your Children Will Eventually Become Like You

Some time during the course of your job as a parent you will come face-to-face with the experience of "you aren't running very much" in your children's lives. Whether you are high EQ or low EQ, you're likely to have such an experience. And, of course, there will be some level of validity to this experience. Nevertheless, the factual nature of the "you aren't running very much" experience will be much more true for low EQ parents. The truth of the matter is that our children grow up to be very much like us. This point is clearly brought home by a short story written by Leo Tolstoy.

THE OLD GRANDFATHER AND THE GRANDSON

The grandfather had become very old. His legs wouldn't go, his eyes didn't see, his ears didn't hear, he had no teeth. And when he ate he dripped from the mouth.

The son and the daughter-in-law stopped setting a place for him at the table and gave him supper in back of the stove. Once they brought dinner down to him in a cup. The old man wanted to move the cup and dropped and broke it. The daughter-in-law began to grumble at the old man for spoiling everything in the house and breaking the cups and said that she would now give him dinner in a dishpan. The old man only sighed and said nothing.

Once the husband and wife were staying at home and watching their small son playing on the floor with some wooden planks; he was building something. The father asked, "What are you doing, Misha?" And Misha said, "Dear Father, I am making you a dishpan. So that when you and dear Mother become old, you may be fed from this dishpan."

The husband and wife looked at each other and began to weep. They became ashamed of so offending the old man, and from then on seated him at the table and waited on him.

A significant number of children who are abused recycle this abuse to their own children. Most importantly, children who are raised in a loving atmosphere become loving, high EQ individuals. Trust the process; it will happen, but probably not as fast as you would like. For example, high EQ parents are more likely to take better care of their physical health via better diet, physical exercise, and other health-promoting measures. But it's pretty unreasonable to expect a sixteen-year-old to eat Grapenuts and jog three miles a day. In similar fashion, it's unreasonable to expect adolescents to be highly motivated to engage in service to others. Trust the foundation you've put down. Our children will eventually become very much like us, whether we like it or not.

> Support your children at all times, even when they make mistakes. Simply be clear that it is they you are supporting and not the mistake.

LITTLE EYES UPON YOU

There are little eyes upon you and they're
watching night and day.
There are little ears that quickly take in every
word you say.
There are little hands all eager
to do anything you do;
And a little boy who's dreaming
of the day he'll be like you.

You're the little fellow's idol,
you're the wisest of the wise.
In his little mind about you
no suspicions ever rise.
He believes in you devoutly,
holds all that you say and do;
He will say and do, in your way,
when he's grown up like you.

There's a wide-eyed little fellow
who believes you're always right;
And his eyes are always opened,
and he watches day and night.
You are setting an example
every day in all you do,
For the little boy who's waiting
to grow up to be like you.

—Anonymous

45

Avoid Fear And Punishment Based Approaches To Behavioral Control

Fear-based discipline results in long-term disaster. In order to use fear, it's necessary that the child be afraid of the parent. Is this the way parents want to be viewed? Fear and punishment require domination. While it's possible for parents to physically dominate their small children, those small children eventually grow up. The years of accumulated resentment that the strapping adolescent is experiencing generally explodes in the form of outright physical rebellion, juvenile delinquency, and/or passive-aggressive behavior.

Our society is quick to employ the techniques of fear. Our religions are fear-based. At the national level our foreign policy is fear-based. The escalation of nuclear arms is the result of fanning the flames of fear. It's important to recognize that no one feels much better with all these nuclear arms around us. At one point, some people went so far as to build underground nuclear shelters in their backyard. I don't believe those people who have personal bomb shelters feel one bit more secure or comforted than the rest of us.

At the Nuremberg Trials, the infamous Nazi, Herman Goering, stated:

> *Why, of course, people don't want war. Why should some poor slob on a farm want to risk his life in a war when the best he can get out of it is to come back to his farm in one piece. Naturally the common people don't want war, neither in Russia, nor in England, nor for that matter in Germany. That is understood. But after all, it is the leaders of a country who determine the*

policy, and it is always a simple matter to drag people along, whether it is a democracy, or a fascist dictatorship, or a parliament, or a communist dictatorship. Voice or no voice, the people can always be brought to the bidding of leaders. That is easy. All you have to do is tell them they are being attacked, and denounce the pacifists for lack of patriotism and exposing the country to danger. It works the same in any country.

Fear doesn't work; fear results in parents being looked upon as aversive agents of punishment, and fear results in low EQ.

In the arena of religion, the belief is that fear is the only thing that can make people tow the line, obey the Ten Commandments. So, we're told that we'll burn in hell if we don't conform. Most don't conform! High EQ people do conform to a high set of standards. In essence, they look at the Ten Commandments and say, "Of course I'll abide by these standards—they simply make sense. Why would I do otherwise when my experience dictates that my life and my relationships are so much more harmonious and pleasant when I abide by these principles?" They follow high standards because they see that the world functions so much better when they do. And they know that the consequences of not following a life of high standards are disharmony, conflict, and a lack of peace of mind. It is this awareness of the nature of things that motivates positive behavior, not fear or guilt.

Some people question this approach, worried that a child who isn't sufficiently punished won't develop a conscience. Conscience is not the same as fear of punishment. Conscience is honoring the feelings and well-being of another *before* one commits a hurtful act, and then restraining oneself from doing so. A person with a good conscience doesn't hurt another because he feels compassion for another's pain. Guilt, on the other hand, occurs *after* one has acted and has been punished. Guilt, as we discussed earlier, rarely changes behavior because it is almost always resolved by psychological defenses such as rationalizing or placing the blame on someone else—most often the victim of one's hurtful behavior. I believe that the best way to encourage a strong conscience in our children is to take an active role in shaping their values through our moment-by-moment actions and words. We must make a commitment ourselves to treat them, and all people, with compassion and to refrain from harmful acts ourselves— regardless of how justified we may feel at the moment. This takes considerably more discipline, planning, and time than a "good whipping," but it is most effective in the long-run.

Spare the rod and spare the child;
Use the rod and spoil the child!

—David Smith

46

Demonstrate A Balance In All Of Life For Your Children

The cornerstones of high Emotional Intelligence are an inner and outer empathy. Healthy EQ means awareness of our physical body, awareness of our mind and its thoughts, awareness of our heart and our feelings, and awareness of the spiritual principles which govern the Universe. Promote this balance and awareness in your life and in the life of your children. Holistic health approaches emphasize harmony between the physical, mental, and spiritual. It's a good practice to frequently assess each of these areas. Is our physical side in harmony with the mental and spiritual? What might improve this balance? Perhaps more exercise, better nutrition, or weight loss. Is the mental side of us in balance? Could we benefit from mental awareness exercises that might reveal self-defeating habitual patterns? What is the state of our spiritual health?

Parents need to make the same assessment of their children. Is their nutrition and exercise level adequate? Do you promote healthy self-cognitions and reinforce positive self-statements? Do you model personal growth efforts, altruism, and service to self and others as part of your spiritual orientation towards life? The balance you demonstrate will be the model they follow.

I learned that if I am to live a spiritual life, I must be able to embody it in every action: in the way I stand and walk, in the way I breathe, in the care with which I eat. All my activities must be included.

—Jack Kornfield,
A Path With Heart

47

Raise Your Children To Be Giraffes

Children lack positive role models. When asked whom they most respect, children list TV personalities, actors, rap singers, or athletes. Shocked adults cite these studies as evidence that today's youth are lacking moral substance. My reaction is that these children are simply reflections of where we, as adults, are placing our attention. How often does a positive person get national or even local media coverage? It's not that there are no positive role models; they are simply lost in the hustle and bustle of everyday life.

Eighteen years ago the Giraffe Project began its efforts to publicly recognize positive role models. The Giraffe Project searches through society for people who, in a sustained way, have "stuck their necks out" to change the social environment or simply the course of an individual life. Once that rarest of creatures is sighted, the project works furiously to publicize the accomplishment and example of each Giraffe, alerting all corners of the media, preparing short publicity spots for radio, spreading a message of good will and optimism that has managed to triumph against all odds.

A Giraffe role model hasn't accomplished just one amazing heroic act, but rather behaves heroically over time. "Many of the nominations we get from all over the country are nominations of wonderful people who have been working tirelessly in a soup kitchen or on an environmental project, or whatever," notes executive director John Graham, whose wife, Ann Medlock, founded the project. "They rarely become Giraffes, because while we honor their work and service, the element of risk isn't prominent enough.

We're looking for the person who had to face down city hall and the neighbors to start the soup kitchen in the first place, someone whose vision and inspiration got other people to join in and build it."

The wondrous work of Giraffes may eventually, through the project's efforts, become well-known, but these stately creatures don't start out famous. According to Mr. Graham, that's what makes them attractive as role models: "So few people can aspire to the level of a Winston Churchill or an Abraham Lincoln. To me, the better role models are rather ordinary people with ordinary gifts, who face extraordinary situations and do extraordinary things."

Not surprisingly, the Giraffe Project focuses much of its energy on young people. "So many kids seem so confused about the distinction between heroes and celebrities," says Mr. Graham. "It's important to let them know that celebrities are people who can hit a home run or are beautiful or play music well, but are not necessarily heroes at all. They're just famous."

Part of its youth-influencing work involves the design of a Standing Tall curriculum for grades K-12 that helps foster courage and caring in students in practical ways. For example, an integral part of the approach is getting kids involved in service activities, which studies show have a measurable impact on reducing negative behavior. Using the powerful imagery of the Giraffe hero profiles, the curriculum seeks to build in young people:

- ◆ courage to take action for the common good;
- ◆ caring for other people, and the ability to empathize across barriers such as culture, race, and age;
- ◆ an enduring, life-guiding vision of responsible citizenship and service to the community;
- ◆ confidence in themselves, and in their abilities to make change happen and to resist and even reverse negative peer pressure;
- ◆ skills in critical thinking, decision-making, leadership, and cooperation.

The students move through three phases of learning:

1. **Hear the Story:** Kids study the acts and lives of Giraffes, learning "how ordinary people can overcome enormous obstacles, and how people who are brave, caring and responsible can lead meaningful and exciting lives." Teachers are also provided with a list of Giraffes willing to visit schools. Such visits are enormously effective, according to the project.

2. **Tell the Story:** With a working definition of a Giraffe, students look for role models in their academic studies and their own communities.

3. **Become the Story:** Finally, students look for Giraffe qualities within themselves and set about designing and implementing community service projects.

Surveying the immensity of the nation's problems, Mr. Graham is as hopeful as one would expect a Giraffe to be. In an article written by Charlie Dodge in *Ethics* (1994/1995), Graham said, "I'm certainly not willing to throw up my hands. I give a lot of speeches and tell stories of these heroes, and I see audiences swept up in the story of these heroes and inspired, and I see the heroes themselves. If more stories of Giraffes come out, if more people were aware of what could be done, if more people had just a bit more conviction in their ideals, we really could turn this around."

We encourage you to start a Giraffe project in your local school, and, better yet, employ the basic principles in your home right now with your family members.

For more information about the Giraffe Project contact: The Giraffe Project, 197 Second Street, P.O. Box 759, Langley, WA 98260, (206) 221-7989.

48

Develop A Self-Awareness Of Your Body

Encourage the development of self-awareness by asking "where" questions, rather than "why" questions. In my practice with clients who come to me complaining of anxiety, I ask them, "How do you know you're anxious?" Most respond by saying they just feel anxious. I ask them what anxiety feels like and just exactly *where* it is. People usually have a great deal of difficulty telling you where their anxiety is. They're confused by questions such as "How big is your anxiety? Is it hot or cold? Where does it begin and end? What color is it? What is the shape of your anxiety?"

Such questions demand the development of self-awareness, especially an awareness of the body and its sensations and feelings. All emotions have a beginning, middle, and end. In the case of anxiety, depression, fear, or anger, we want the middle to be as short as possible. But what we do—and don't do—generally drags the middle out rather than brings it to an end.

What we do is try to resist the emotion rather than open to it. "What you resist will persist" is particularly relevant with emotions. Resist depression and it will persist. Resist anxiety and it will persist. Resistance of anxiety means not being willing to feel it. Nonresistance means asking where the anxiety is. Ask yourself, "What exactly does this thing I call anxiety feel like and exactly where is it?" This will result in the emotion moving through you rather than staying stuck in you.

When your children come to you and say they feel tired, hungry, or mad, use these situations as opportunities to develop self-awareness. Children love to describe colors, temperatures, sizes, shapes, weights, even the tastes and smells of their feelings. It helps them soothe themselves, but it also provides acknowledgment of what they feel in the presence of a safe and loving parent.

As parents, we're often threatened by our children's feelings. When they feel bad, we often feel inadequate or wrong. At the very least we feel their pain. How often do we tell a crying child that his skinned knee doesn't really hurt, or a frustrated teenager that he really isn't bored in school? This tells the child that he must feel differently in order to please us. The end result is a sense of not knowing what one really feels and numbing to the sensations of the body. We shouldn't really be surprised if the child grows up baffled by feelings such as love or grief.

So give your children permission to explore their feelings. Develop this capacity early and you will have fostered the growth of a primary ingredient of sound psychological health and high EQ, that is, of self-awareness.

To live in this precious animal body on this earth is as great a part of spiritual life as anything else.

—Jack Kornfield

49

Children Must Understand That Love Is A Choice

The popular notion of romantic love, which lasts forever, exists in the movies and pulp romance magazines; it is not a fact of real life. After the fire of romantic love wanes, as it always must, the mature couple *chooses* to love each other. Until that choice is made no real love existed. Most never make that choice because they don't know the choice even exists.

The high EQ person chooses to behave lovingly even when he doesn't feel like it. When people behave exactly the way they feel like behaving all the time, they usually end up in prison. To not yell when we feel like yelling, to not hit when we feel like hitting, and to talk things out when we feel like leaving are all strong signs of good emotional management.

> Each day offers an opportunity to choose your partner and your children—to love them and to choose to celebrate these relationships.

There is a love like a small lamp which goes out when the oil is consumed; or like a stream which dries up when it doesn't rain. But there is a love that is like a mighty spring gushing up out of the earth; it keeps flowing forever, and is inexhaustible.

—Isaac of Nineveh

50

Avoid The Tendency To Compare

The mind loves to compare things. It seeks happiness through comparing. Yet the real results of these comparisons are false pride, jealousy, envy, disappointment, competition, and pretending as if we wish others well, when we really don't want them to have it better than we do. The mechanism of comparison pits us against other people, and there is no aliveness in being against others. Aliveness comes from being *for* other people and recognizing that when they make it we make it.

With regard to our own children, the mind compares them to the ideal image we've created and pictured in our head. Who could ever live up to that ideal image? The relationship with our children suffers a loss of love every time we compare them to our ideal. In the case of my own son, I wanted a 6'4" All-American quarterback who starred at Notre Dame. He would score at the genius level on IQ tests. He would get his medical degree from Harvard, and he never would forget to give me 100 percent of the credit for his success. Of course his favorite foods, beginning in early childhood, would have been spinach, broccoli, carrots, liver, and raw fruits. Children can never measure up to the inflated set of ideals most of us have for them.

The second and even more devastating kind of comparison we make is with other children. Is my child smarter than the neighbor's child? Who gets the best grades? Is my daughter a cheerleader? Is she more attractive and the envy of other parents and their daughters? Do my children have special qualities that earmark them as unique and better than other kids? Do they have strong spiritual inclinations that set them apart from other children?

All these comparisons make us highly critical of our children. We're always trying to change them and hoping they'll be different. When we're in this frame of reference, it's as if our children are here exclusively for our purpose, to bring us the recognition we never had or a renewal of the recognition that has tarnished with age. Somehow they are supposed to make us what we could not fully be ourselves. Again, our children are doomed to fail us when we constantly compare them to others. The result is a constant nagging for our children to be different. All of our interactions with them occur within the context of them needing to change and be better. It's little wonder that the quality and quantity of communication diminishes significantly as our children get older.

It is vital that we accept our children and love them exactly as they are. And who they most fundamentally are is a child who has been given to us by God. No matter how far from the truth this may seem to be sometimes, it is, nevertheless, absolutely true. And whenever this vital fact is forgotten, love is diminished and the bond between parent and child suffers.

With both your words and your actions, let your children know they are a child of God and that God doesn't make any defective materials. Remind them continually that they are the sunshine of the Spirit and that there's a flame within them that delights in bringing joy to others. It is in this fundamental sense that we are all so much more alike than we are different. Since it's sometimes difficult to see the light of the Spirit, it's important that we make it our expressed purpose to never forget that it is always there. If we can stay focused on this light-spirit, our communications with our children will always be heard because they'll be heart-to-heart rather than head-to-head.

I've found it valuable to talk to my son about the comparisons my mind makes. When I bring them out into the light, they become a little smaller and less likely to reoccur. These comparisons have become a considerable source of humor because of their preposterous nature. I always make sure that my son knows the ridiculous and meaningless nature of these comparisons, and that I love him unconditionally. He knows there is nothing he could ever do that would challenge my love for him or dim the light of his spirit. When children know this, they simply do not do the things that test our love.

The Kahlil Gibran poem entitled "Children" is a beautiful reminder of the true nature of our children and our role as parents.

CHILDREN

Your children are not your children.
They are the sons and daughters of Life's longing for itself.
They come through you but not from you,
And though they are with you,
yet they belong not to you.

You may give them your love but not your thoughts,
For they have their own thoughts.
You may house their bodies but not their souls,
For their souls dwell in the house of tomorrow, which you cannot visit, not even in your dreams.
You may strive to be like them, but seek not to make them like you.
For life goes not backwards nor tarries with yesterday.

You are the bows from which your children as living arrows are sent forth.
The archer sees the mark upon the path of the infinite, and He bends you with His might that His arrows may go swift and far.
Let your bending in the archer's hand be for gladness;
For even as He loves the arrow that flies,
so He loves also the bow that is stable.

<u>51</u>

Create A Calm And Serene Atmosphere

A peaceful home environment can be a vital contribution to your child's EQ level. Avoiding loud music, eliminating the constant drone of meaningless television programs, and maintaining a calm tone of voice even during times of disharmony (especially during times of disharmony!) can greatly add to the warmth and peaceful nature of your child and the home environment.

It's not easy to maintain your cool during times of disagreement. I've already mentioned the importance of affectionate physical contact during times of distress. If it takes attending classes that are designed to promote anger management or "peaceful conflict," then please do so. Remember that your children's interactions and conflict resolution skills will very likely imitate the ones you consistently demonstrate to them. Is this good news?

If you're dissatisfied with the model you've presented to your children, tell them your concerns and clearly specify how you want to behave in the future. Actively enlist their assistance. Let them know you value their input. Also let them know that you're willing to attend classes, if necessary, that will promote the harmony you want to experience and model for them. Tell them that they are worth the effort and so is the family relationship. When you speak this way to your children, and behave consistent with your word, your children will know you value them, and they will value themselves—and you.

In the face of man-made calamity that every war is, one must affirm and reaffirm, again and again, that the waging of war is not inevitable or un-changeable. Humanity is not destined to self-de-struction. Clashes of ideologies, aspirations and needs can and must be settled and resolved by means other than war and violence.

—Pope John Paul II

<u>52</u>

TeachYour Children To Bring Forth That Which Is Inside OfThem

Jesus said, "If you bring forth that which is inside of you, what you bring forth will save you. If you do not bring forth that which is inside of you, what you do not bring forth will destroy you."

I believe that Jesus was stressing the importance of bringing forth our natural desire to love and connect with other people and to experience that we make a difference in their lives. If these natural tendencies are not allowed to flourish and come forth, they will fester inside and result in disharmony and dis-ease. First and foremost, we must love and connect with our children at a deep spiritual level. They will then recognize that they make a difference in our lives. Their natural inclination will then be to pass this love and connectedness on to others and to experience that they make a difference in the world. Do everything you must do to bring this forth from your children. A high level of EQ is impossible without the sense that your presence on the planet makes a difference.

There is a tremendous sense of satisfaction that comes when we consider our children to be our greatest accomplishment. But let's not stop there. Let's take everyone to the top.

53

The Lack Of Humor In The Average Household Is No Laughing Matter

The joy of hearing the laughter of children is truly a spiritual event. Unfortunately, I am struck by the lack of humor and genuine laughter that exists in many households. Numerous research articles have clearly outlined the psychological and physiological benefits of smiling and laughing. Medical research suggests that laughter improves the immune system; and many people believe they have literally cured themselves of terminal illness with humor alone.

My belief is that the spirit is also uplifted when the family can join together in laughter. Create situations in which this is possible—and don't be afraid to giggle along with the children as they watch the slapstick comedy of the Three Stooges.

I think the family can cure much of its ills by actively practicing the art of humor. So be sure not to dampen your child's natural inclination towards laughter. And always be sure that the humor is victimless and not at the expense of someone else. Of course, laughing at ourselves is the best humor of all. Humor and high EQ go hand in hand. I'm told that God has a fantastic sense of humor. And I also suspect He has an extremely high EQ.

True humor is fun—it does not
put down, kid, or mock.
It makes people feel wonderful,
not separate, different and cut off.
True humor has beneath it the understanding
that we are all in this together.

—Hugh Prather

Mirth is like a flash of lightning
that breaks through a gloom of clouds,
and glitters for a moment;
Cheerfulness keeps up a kind of daylight in the mind,
and fills it with a steady and perpetual serenity.

—Joseph Addison

54

We Are All In This Together

Let your children know we're all in this thing called Life together, and either we're all going to make it or none of us is going too make it.

At some time fairly early on in life, most of us develop the crazy idea that we'll be thought of more highly if someone else is thought of less highly. This faulty belief is the source of jealousy, resentment, unhealthy competition, gossip, put-downs, betrayals, judgments, and hidden agendas. It is what's behind our usually well disguised hope that other people don't get ahead of us in the game of Life. We don't want someone else to make it because somehow we have it made up that if they make it, we don't.

The truth of the matter is that we're all in this arena of Life together, and it is all in our best interests to lend a helping hand. Our mind may have the belief that it's a dog-eat-dog-world, but dogs don't eat other dogs. Our belief may also be that we must look out for Number One at all costs. But just looking out for myself is a very lonely way to live. It is when I'm willing to extend myself to others that I feel most alive. Extend yourself to your children and to others, and they will learn this valuable lesson.

The fact is that we in the United States are already "ahead" of most of humankind. How does this make us feel? What are we supposed to do now that we're "ahead"? We're in the same predicament as the dog that chases the car and finally catches it. "What now?" must be his thoughts too.

The world would be better off
If people tried to be better.
And people would become better
If they stopped trying to be better off.

For when everybody tries to become better off,
Nobody is better off.
But when everybody tries to become better,
Everybody is better off.

—Peter Maurin, Catholic Worker Movement

Only a life lived for others is worth living.

—Albert Einstein

55

Let Your Children Know That Things Are Not Always The Way They Appear To Be

We are told by informed sources that the Earth is rotating on its axis at about 1000 miles per hour, that it is revolving around the Sun at the speed of almost one million miles per day, and that our whole solar system is being jettisoned into space at an almost unbelievable rate of speed. None of this appears to be the case to our limited senses. Life has many great mysteries. How did we get here? Where are we going? What happens after death? Most of us have beliefs about the answers to these questions, but even the most fervent of us are likely to have some doubts and anxiety.

Several years ago I was jogging down a lonely country road that was flanked on each side by a traditional three-tiered barbed-wire fence. As I glanced over to one side I noticed that a young deer was hanging upside down with its rear leg securely caught between two twisted tiers of the fence. The deer had been unable to wiggle free from this predicament and had hung there upside down until it had died. As I took in this scene I became furious. I looked up to the heavens and demanded some explanation for what appeared to me to be such an unnecessary and senseless act of misery. There was simply no way to make any sense of this situation. As minor as this episode may seem to someone else, it was a significant emotional event for me and represented a sort of spiritual crisis. I wanted so badly to know how and why a loving Supreme Force would allow this to happen. After a great deal of psychological distress, I simply decided that "I don't know!" This was not just a casual "I don't know," but one that I felt in the depth of my heart. Interestingly, it was accompanied by the certainty that things were not at all what they sometimes appeared to be. I felt sure that there was much more to the apparent unfairness and misery in Life than I was privileged to understand. Additionally, I felt certain that at some time in the future I would be privileged to every bit of information I ever had any questions about, and it would all make sense with pristine clarity. Until that time comes I will continually remind myself that Life is simply not what it appears to be to my senses sometimes, and I will trust in the great mystery that surrounds us all.

Teach your children about this great mystery. Talk about it with them. Provide them with a spiritual orientation and have playful discussions about the mystery. Let them know that they'll be provided with all the answers, perhaps even within this lifetime. Let your children know that there's much more to Life than a quick trip from the hospital's maternity ward to the cemetery. Life doesn't begin with birth nor does it end with death. Life isn't an evolutionary fluke that is simply a brief meaningless flash between the darkness of pre-birth and the nothingness of post-death. And Life isn't a testing ground that will result in most of the contestants being doomed to an eternity of misery, while a few who behave appropriately get rewarded with everlasting bliss. I know it isn't that way!

Almost every religious tradition fosters the idea that what we see is not really reality. Many also suggest that every single human being is going to make it in a heavenly sense. I strongly encourage us to promote this "we are all going to make it" perspective to our children. I believe it will allow them to live more harmoniously and with a greater sense of justice, mercy, self-worth, self-esteem, and compassion.

Appearances to the mind are of four kinds. Things either are what they appear to be; or they neither are, nor appear to be; or they are and do not appear to be; or they are not, and yet appear to be. Rightly to aim in all these cases is the wise man's task.

—Epictetus

56

Teach Your Children How To Pray

Many of us don't know how to pray. This inability is painfully evident even though our society is becoming aware of the scientific proof of the effectiveness of prayer for the healing of mind, body, and spirit. Fifty years ago the miracle of antibiotics did wonders for bodily ailments and diseases such as polio, tuberculosis, and the flu. At that time we also became aware of body deficiencies involving certain vitamins and minerals. These discoveries greatly assisted with the elimination of many of the catastrophic physical ailments that hindered humankind. However, such developments did little to affect our psychological health. Patients continued to visit their physician with complaints of stress, tension, psychosomatic issues, depression, and anxiety. Medicine, psychiatry, and psychology responded to these non-physical problems with stress reduction techniques—meditation, relaxation, and a host of psychotherapeutic practices. While these methods have resulted in some relief, the results have rarely been completely successful.

The latest attempt to provide relief for psychological discomfort is sometimes called psycho-spiritual. It is an outgrowth of the increasing scientific awareness that prayer and the depth of one's spiritual faith have a great deal to do with both psychological and physical health. The "depth of one's spiritual faith" that I'm speaking of far transcends the rigid religious fundamentalism that is so often characterized by prejudice, in-group superiority, dogmatism, and the promotion of rampant fear.

Given the evolution of psycho-spirituality and the scientific community's awareness of the value of prayer, just how does one actually pray? I would like to offer a model for prayer. It's just a suggested model—one of many good ones that are available. It uses the "**A-C-T-S H-O-W**" acronym.

The "**A**" stands for adoration. It just seems appropriate to start out by honoring the Higher Power with the recognition of magnificence.

The "**C**" stands for confession. Simple enough! Just state what it is you are sorry for and commit to working towards a life that eliminates that activity.

The "**T**" represents thanksgiving. This involves giving thanks for life itself and for the many benefits that one receives almost daily.

The "**S**" means solicitation. Solicitation involves making a request. This request may be for oneself or for someone or something else. The request might be that you be shown God's will for you.

That covers the **A-C-T-S** of prayers. The **H-O-W** involves honesty (**H**), open-mindedness (**O**), and willingness (**W**).

Collectively, "ACTS HOW" is one of the models for prayer you may use and teach to your children.

> *It is only at the end of this world that we shall realize how the destinies of persons and nations have been shaped, not so much by the external actions of powerful men and by the events that seemed inevitable, but by the quiet, silent, irresistible prayer of persons the world will never know.*
>
> —Anthony de Mello, S.J.

57

Beware Of Your Children Becoming Adults

In the minds of children nothing is impossible. Any idea that they can't or shouldn't do something is the result of our input into their minds. Of course, some of our input is valuable and may even have survival value for them. Unfortunately, a great deal of what we pour into a child's mind gradually, but significantly, restricts their behavior and thinking as they grow older. Clearly, young children have a great deal of fun much of the time. Adults don't—in part because they're so busy preparing to have fun!

What is it that gradually happens between the ages of five and twenty-five that accounts for this difference? Undoubtedly, many factors are involved. But I believe a large portion of the problem is that parents incorporate dark, unproductive, and restrictive thoughts into their children's minds, and that voice becomes their children's internal voice. Children constantly hear "don't get dirty, put your shoes on, stay out of the mud, don't get caught in the rain, be careful, bundle up and stay warm, watch out for strangers, get home early, save your money, be somebody (who?), don't eat all that junk," etc., etc. We impose so many restrictions that it's little wonder adulthood is viewed as serious as a heart attack. But if life isn't fun, what's the point? If we can't play in the rain and "squish" our toes in the mud because of "What would other adults think?", what have we given up? If we won't go to the beach because we think we're too fat to be seen in a bathing suit, who suffers from this self-imposed restriction? And if we don't go out to a restaurant or a movie by ourselves because everybody else is there with someone, where does that leave us?—home, alone, and bored.

The average adult has so many unrecognized restrictions floating around in his head that it's little surprise there are so few childlike pleasures left in his behavioral repertoire.

So don't restrict your children with unnecessary cultural or age-related limitations. Encourage them to run and play in the rain, to go barefoot in the grass, and to be their own decision-makers. A rule of thumb in our house is that if it doesn't hurt anybody else or oneself, it's probably O.K. to do. So go for a walk in the rain, feel the cool wetness on your face, eat some Ben and Jerry's ice cream, recognize your need for aliveness, and promote the same with your children.

Except ye be converted and become as little children,
ye shall not enter into the kingdom of heaven.

—Jesus

58

Teach Your Children The Basics Of Life

I don't know exactly what the ideal holistic education should look like, but I'm sure it goes far beyond what is taught in our public schools. Until our schools catch up, I think it is our responsibility to assist our children to function more capably in our current world.

With this is mind, I think every child should have the confidence and self-assuredness that comes with knowing how to endure in the wilderness. Whether we are lost, snowed in, hurt, or stranded, the art of wilderness survival—which requires experience, know-how, calculated judgment, and a sense of confidence—is something we should all know.

Additionally, we should all be acquainted with shelter building, basic carpentry, food growing techniques, clothes making, some form of martial art, and basic interpersonal relationship skills. It's up to us as parents to teach these basic skills to our children, or to ensure that they receive them beginning at an early age.

In making these recommendations, I'm not promoting a survival mentality but rather a confidence mentality. If we're to regard ourselves highly, it will likely be due to our reflections regarding our accomplishments and the sense we have regarding our ability to handle all of life's adversities.

So have your fifteen-year-old daughter (and son) change a tire before they drive by themselves. While explaining the rationale underlying this seemingly foolish request, don't promote a fear orientation, but one of confidence. Low EQ is a fear-based perspective. Don't tell your children they need to learn to fix a tire because someone will stop and molest or harm them. Despite what the six o'clock news reports may convey to us, the chances of this happening are really miniscule. The issue is one of helplessness versus competency. Promote competency and don't burden your children with exaggerated fear and survival concerns. They're bombarded with enough of that elsewhere. Instilling survival concerns erodes the spirit of aliveness that is so prevalent in our young children.

You have already survived!
Much of what you do to guarantee this survival is redundant and wasted selfish energy that does not contribute to the quality of your life.

59

Let Your Children Know They Are The Perfect Vessel That Holds It All

Let your children know they are different from all the things going on in their lives. At any one time there is a whole multitude of external factors that compete for our attention. Each of these factors has a certain potential to upset our peace, centeredness, and harmony. There are money matters, relationship and marital concerns, aging parents, job problems, and numerous other issues that are physically external yet become internalized psychologically. Each factor can demand our attention and scream loudly into our mind until we focus on it and it "becomes" us.

But these things going on in our lives aren't really us at all. These external events are the content of our lives, and our lives will always have content. Moreover, our lives will always, to some degree, have content that we don't like or want. In large measure, we don't have control over our life's content. We can't control automobile breakdowns, when our parents and loved ones might die, natural disasters that may affect us, or even whether our spouse will leave us for someone else. But all these things are not who we are—they're merely the content of life we must deal with. And we aren't the content; we're the entity that holds all this content. The content is like the gumballs in a gumball machine. The glass vessel that holds all the gumballs is the crucial entity. The gumballs may be damaged and imperfect, but the glass vessel that holds the content is whole and complete and perfect. Don't confuse who you are with the content of your life. Every human being, regardless of the content he has in his life, is whole and complete and perfect. You are not your divorce; you are that which holds your divorce. You are not your money problems; you are that which holds your money problems. We must remember neither to "become" our divorce nor to "become" our money issues.

So teach your children who they are: not the stuff that is going on in their lives, but the perfect vessel that holds all of that stuff. This shift in awareness of who they really are can greatly assist them to recognize the passing nature of external events and the permanent nature of the perfect God-created self that is the witness of it all.

Knowing who we are requires us to look inside
rather than outside.

60

Help Your Children Take Life Lightly

Given the fact that we're all going to die, and that we all have to live until we die, it's best not to take this thing called Life too seriously.

Several months ago my wife taught me a very valuable lesson. I was trying to scoop some ice out of the icemaker and spilled six or seven cubes on the kitchen floor. The numbers of swear words I uttered almost exceeded the number of spilled cubes. My wife, who was a witness to this scene, looked at me and matter-of-factly asked, "Why is that so important?" Before my mind could think, my heart got the message. Ice cubes on the floor are not at all important and are hardly worth giving up my centeredness and peace. Most of our upsets are about unimportant things, and I'm constantly amazed at how little it takes to upset my peace—even after what feels like a lifetime of work in this area.

We simply must remember, and teach our children to remember, that there is a dramatic difference between a lump in the gravy, a lump in the throat, and a lump in a lymph gland.

It's often said that angels can fly because they take themselves and the events of the world lightly. Promote this lightness in your children. Life should not be continually viewed as being as serious as a heart attack. This type of thinking will promote one. Don't burden your children with heavy, serious thoughts about tragedy and survival and being somebody in life. In case you haven't noticed, they already have survived and they already are somebody. And so are you!

Try not to become a person of success,
but rather a person of value.

—Albert Einstein

61

Keep Things Simple

A famous saying attributed to Gandhi is "Live simply, so that others may simply live." This statement has ramifications on various levels: the individual level, the family level, and the community/world level. For the individual, living simply has many personal benefits. Instead of living simply, though, we try to collect as many things as we can—cars, money, houses, clothes, retirement accounts, mechanical devices, expensive toys—all of which clutter up our lives and eventually seem to be more of a complication than a source of satisfaction. The middle-class child collects so many toys that it takes two hours every night just to pick them up. And yet for children who have no toys at all, tin cans, sticks, and string seem to result in just as much fun as the array of latest action figures and expensive gadgets. Christmas can be a perplexing and frustrating time for parents who watch their children anxiously go from present to present, spending only a brief moment with each before moving on to the next. Finally, they settle down with their favorite gift and generally give the rest of them a minimal amount of attention.

There is, of course, a price to pay for all the stuff adults and children accumulate. Firstly, we must work to pay for all that stuff. Secondly, it must all be stored, maintained, insured, worried about, dragged around, sold at a garage sale, or paid to be hauled away. Finally, and of most importance, there is the realization that having all this stuff doesn't equate with more contentment in our lives. Many adults have noticed that possessions literally exhaust us. Certainly, a child's happiness is hardly correlated with the amount of toys he has.

So let your children see you living a simple life. Help them recognize that people who have everything they want aren't any happier than those without all the external trappings of success. Let them know that if they go through life trying to satisfy their *wants*, they are doomed to frustration and failure. Also let them know that it is quite simple to go through life satisfying their *needs*. Adults, and even fairly young children, can learn and recognize that it is simply impossible to get enough of what you don't need. Some people spend a lifetime trying.

The problem, of course, is that for human beings desire is almost endless. We see something, it completely occupies our mind, and everything else is secondary. We don't have to be in a toy store with our children very long to experience this situation. But we adults are not much different, perhaps just a little more self-contained. A rule of thumb in our household is to try to wait seventy-two hours before satisfying the desire to buy some new toy. Almost always, the intensity of the desire has greatly diminished and we're able to see things much more clearly.

There must be more to life than having everything.

—Maurice Sendak

To pretend to satisfy one's desires by possessions is like putting out a fire with straw.

—Chinese proverb

62

Teach Your Children The Importance Of Intentions

This sounds very simple. Why should we teach our children to be aware of their intentions? *Simply because everyone always gets exactly what he intends to get!* This is a difficult concept to understand because much of what we intend occurs just outside of the realm of our usual awareness. It took me many years to recognize that I would somehow start an argument with my wife on those nights that we had a planned activity and I really didn't want to go. The payoff was that I didn't have to go out. The cost was argumentation, bad feelings, a missed opportunity for intimacy, and the experience of anger instead of love. You might notice that the cost outweighs the payoff. This often goes unrecognized because our intentions aren't clear. Most of us deny that we had any intention to start an argument, get a divorce, get fired, get depressed, and so forth. It takes awareness to avoid being victimized by yourself. We must begin with openness to ourselves as being the *creator* of our experience. Without openness and awareness, what we say we want, and what we really intend, are often quite different things. The first few lines of Nelson Mandela's 1994 inaugural speech tells us:

Our deepest fear is not that we are inadequate. Our deepest fear is that we are powerful beyond belief.

Can it be that we intend to be inadequate to avoid our deepest fear that we are powerful beyond belief? We all say we want to be powerful, but our intention may be contrary—and we always get exactly what we intend.

So help your children voice their intentions early on in life—

because we will all get exactly what we intend. (For an excellent explanation of intentionality, see *Winning Through Enlightenment* by Ron Smothermon, M.D.)

ROAD TO HEAVEN

Before leaving the subject of intention, let me mention a rampant myth and hopefully set it to rest. It is often said that "The road to hell is paved with good intentions." This is absolutely false. First of all, the road to hell is not even paved. Secondly, not only is it not paved, it doesn't even exist. There are no roads that lead to hell. All roads lead to Heaven! Now, some of the roads that lead to Heaven are extremely long and bumpy as hell, but no matter what road you take, you'll eventually get to Heaven. It may take some of us a very, very long time to get there, perhaps many lifetimes; but we will all, every single one of us, get there eventually. And we'll all have a grand celebration that will include a belly laugh that lasts beyond forever. Let your children know this and never forget it yourself!

63

Honesty—A Real Dilemma

I honestly don't have the answer to honesty. Whenever I think I do, a situation comes up and I recognize that I don't. For example, what should your children do when they find someone physically unattractive and that person asks them for an assessment of their physical appearance? Should they tell the truth? Should they "fudge" at least a little bit? Should they withhold the truth completely? Should they make an assessment of that person's ability to deal with the truth and let that assessment dictate what they say? Should they outright lie and not take a chance on hurting the person's feelings?

Let's explore some of the options we have with regard to honesty.

Option 1: Always tell the truth as you see it. This sounds simple enough. But what if your sensitive sixty-five-year-old mother asks you how she looks in the new orange dress you know she loves? With this option you must tell her she looks like a fat pumpkin and that you hope no one notices that she is your mother. With this option, if you're asked to express your opinion, you must "tell it like it is." This option does have the possibility of working out just fine. The only problem is that both people have to be enlightened, or nearly so.

There is little doubt that sometimes the truth can hurt someone. Of course, it is vital that we never intentionally try to hurt someone with the truth. The truth told for this sake is worse than any lie.

Option 2: Tell people what will make them feel good. When your son shows you the drawing of a house and tree he made during third-grade art class, is there really any sense in telling him that the picture displays precious little artistic talent? I think not.

My inclination here is to say, "Sweetheart, I'm your dad and I love it, and I love the tiny little fingers that have drawn it, too."

I use this option with my wife sometimes and she uses it with me. Unless some sort of public or social embarrassment is imminent, I might "fudge" the truth to some degree and tell her I had a good time during the evening we had out, even if I was frequently preoccupied with a work deadline.

Option 3: Consider spiritual growth. M. Scott Peck, in his best-selling book, *The Road Less Traveled*, has an excellent chapter called "Withholding Truth." While Peck condones withholding the truth, it is only under very limited circumstances, and each case must involve a well-examined moral decision, empathic rather than self-serving ends, love for the other person, and an assessment of how the truth would affect the spiritual growth of the other person. Peck also believes that we should never speak any falsehood.

As my own spiritual growth progresses, I find myself drawn more and more to Peck's perspective. Although I am aiming for spiritual perfection, I believe I'll have to settle for spiritual progress. I hope someday to live this option more fully to the letter.

Clearly, honesty presents us with a real moral dilemma. If we struggle with the concept of honesty, I believe that, in itself, indicates a high level of emotional and spiritual intelligence. While honesty is not situational, each situation will present a different array of issues to wrestle with. Talk openly about the dilemma of honesty with your children. Let them see the moral struggle it presents to you, and help them with the many decisions they'll have to make regarding honesty in their childhood, teen, and adult years.

The truth knows when to speak and when not to
—anything else is a manipulation.
—Bryon Katie Rolle

A truth is to be known always, to be uttered sometimes.
—Kahlil Gibran

<u>64</u>

Never Make Your Child
Or Anyone Else Wrong

It sounds almost impossible, doesn't it? And why not tell someone they're wrong when they are? The problem is that whenever you make someone wrong, the only message that persons gets is that you are making him wrong. Nothing else gets through, and what you have is an argument, perhaps even a silent one, but certainly not communication.

So do whatever you must, say whatever you must, but don't make the person wrong. Clearly, the spirit of what you do is the issue here. In the natural order of things, one might argue that there is no right or wrong. But the Universe certainly has *consequences* for certain ways of behaving. Point out these consequences without making your child wrong. A child isn't wrong for not sharing his toys—and there *are* consequences. Lying isn't wrong, and there are big nasty consequences, one of them being that people will avoid you like the plague once you've been exposed often enough. And being exposed happens soon enough because it's one of the natural consequences. Sticking with consequences and avoiding making your child wrong eliminates blame, guilt, shame, argumentation, and self-esteem issues that often increase the undesired behavior.

Our task as parents is to consistently point out the consequences to our children in a loving non-judgmental way. This can be difficult, however, when our child's behavior is embarrassing or frustrating to us. Toddlers who throw tantrums in department stores and teenagers who argue about our most reasonable house rules are each a case in point. How easy it is to take the short-term solution and spank them, call them names, or send them out of our sight with a look of disgust. A long-term solution is to point out the consequences for their behavior—which sometimes requires creative thinking, and always takes a great deal of effort and persistence. I believe that many parents settle for the short-term option early on in their child's life because they themselves lack the discipline to appropriately manage consequences. And the unfortunate consequence for the parent's behavior is an out-of-control teenager who hardly cares whether you call him names, love him, or look at him at all.

So make the effort to consistently point out the consequences of your child's behavior. With time, your effort will be rewarded with a healthy, self-confident, and self-disciplined child. With sufficient awareness, why would anyone choose anger over harmony, selfishness over sharing, hatred over kindness and love? Anger, selfishness, and hatred are, in and of themselves, painful consequences.

When you judge people, you have no time to love them.

—Mother Teresa

<u>65</u>

The Importance Of Nonverbal Communication

Verbal communication is overrated. Much of what we really want to convey is beyond words. All languages have a lot of words that label our feelings, but frequently they miss the mark. The headache I may have is very difficult to describe to someone else. I might assume someone else's headache is just like mine, yet each of us is unique. I might say that my pain feels as though there's someone inside my head banging my brain with a hammer. These words really aren't very accurate, but they're the best way we can explain things sometimes.

Often it is simply best to communicate with physical touch. This is especially true with children and spouses when negative turmoil and anger may be involved. With both our children and our spouses, we often intend to communicate peacefully, but we often simply reenact old automatic behavioral patterns. Then anger, frustration, and yelling emerge. Healing, reconciliation, and renewed bonding are impossible when anger is present.

During my twenty-year tenure as a psychologist within the Federal Bureau of Prisons, I became acquainted with a warden who had a unique method of dealing with employees who couldn't get along. He simply told them to go into the conference room together and not come out until they had a smile on their faces and the problem was resolved. Of course, this warden was expecting them to deal with their issues with verbal communication. My solution is to hug each other until you are both able to let go of the negativity and existing inner turmoil. I wasn't courageous enough to suggest this method with two hostile employees. But I do know it's what works best with our children and our spouses. Just keep on hugging until the love overcomes the negativity. It's best to agree to use this as a procedure before adverse situations arise. It's important to recognize that you probably won't feel like hugging the other person during times of strife, but if you honestly give this technique a try it will work for you. When using this method with loved ones, it works best to lie or sit down together and to embrace each other as fully and as completely as possible. Simply maintain this contact until you're able to say, "I love you." Don't add anything to the "I love you." If tears come, as they often will, allow them to be there along with your expression of love.

Where words fail, it's comforting to realize how many other vital and eloquent ways we have of communicating with each other.

—Leo Buscaglia,
Bus 9 to Paradise

<u>66</u>

Let Your Children Know There Is A Power Even Greater Than Mom And Dad

Our children will eventually need a spiritual component to make sense of their lives. Young children are naturally spiritual. They're in awe of everything, inquisitive about the mysteries of life and quick to find joy in things that adults hardly even notice.

This curiosity with the Universe often fades as the teenage years approach. Yet it is during these teenage years that children struggle with the most fundamental spiritual issues—such as how to reconcile the complexities of living, and what to do with the gift of life that has been given to them. At the same time they become painfully aware that Mom and Dad are simply human beings, which creates both vulnerability and cynicism. These can be challenging times, and they are likely to take a great toll on both parents and child if a solid and firm spiritual groundwork hasn't been put into place during early childhood.

Children need spiritual ideals. These ideals help them to look inward in search of meaning and purpose. They help them to discover what really matters in life, to cope with loss, to connect with others, and to guide their behavior from day to day. In addition, this need for spiritual guidance will be with them throughout the course of their lives, even if they fail to recognize it.

It will be easier for the child to embrace spirituality in later years if he was made aware of the fact that there is a Power bigger than both Mom and Dad. How you wish to explain and describe this Power is up to you. For those of you who have difficulty with traditional religion, it may simply suffice to repeatedly affirm the existence of a Higher Power to your children. Read stories and poems, and discuss the mysteries of life. They will get the message if you live it.

Wherever two or more are gathered in my name,
there am I in the midst of them.

—Jesus

I can see... in what you call the dark,
but which to me is golden. I can see a God-made world,
not a man-made world.

—Helen Keller

<u>67</u>

Teach Your Children About Resentments And How They Can Erode One's Physical, Mental, And Spiritual Well-being

We hold resentments against people who don't treat us the way we think we should be treated. Our self-image gets bruised, or our ambitions get thwarted, or we become fearful of losing something (such as money, reputation, security, or companions).

Generally, we rehearse our grudges against others over and over again, and often verbalize them to our friends, who are likely to automatically agree with our point of view and thereby fan the flames. Unfortunately, a life full of resentments blocks our experience of happiness and spirituality. Therefore, it is important that we teach our children a method to regularly clear out their accumulated resentments. To be sure, there are times when we will be treated poorly or unfairly. Yet almost always, if we're willing to closely examine the situation, we can find something that we contributed to the event that somehow affected the other person's behavior. The task is to painstakingly discover how we were at fault, and to notice what part of our ego was bruised and contributory. Did our fear, selfishness, pride, desire for power, need to be in control, security concerns, financial issues, or desire to impress others get in the way? We need to discover how we contributed to the event so that what is learned can be applied to future situations. Over time we'll see a pattern of issues that interfere with our interactions with others. These patterns are most clearly in evidence with our children and spouse. This knowledge, when applied to future situations, is wisdom.

I recommend that each evening before bedtime family members ask themselves, "Did I treat anyone unkindly today? If so, can I make amends? What acts of kindness did I perform today?

What do I intend to do tomorrow to be more spiritual?" These questions should first be asked with regard to others in the family, then extended to others we had contact with throughout the day.

> *Each person is like an actor who wants to run the whole show; is forever trying to arrange the lights, the ballet, the scenery and the rest of the players in his own way. If his arrangements would only stay put, if people would do as he wished, the show would be great. Everyone, including himself, would be pleased. Life would be wonderful... What usually happens? The show doesn't come off very well. He begins to think life doesn't treat him right... Admitting he may be somewhat at fault, he is sure that other people are more to blame. He becomes angry, indignant, self-pitying.*

—Alcoholics Anonymous

> *When evil men plot, good men must plan; When evil men shout ugly words of hatred, good men must commit themselves to the glory of love.*

—Martin Luther King, Jr.

<u>68</u>

Good Parents Are Rewarded With Nose Prints On The Glass

Someone once told me that good parents know who they are because of the nose prints on the glass. How you greet your children has a lot to do with how they'll eventually come to greet you. Make a special effort to ensure that the initial interchange is full of warmth and love.

This may be difficult. Often, we're too preoccupied to take advantage of those routine yet precious moments with our children. After driving an hour through congested traffic, rehearsing an argument with a boss, or thinking about dinner, we're hardly in the proper mood to greet our children with joy. Instead, we charge into the house and point out that the bicycle was left in the driveway once again!

When I'm in this mood, I try to remember an excerpt from a book by Robert Fulghum entitled *Everything I Really Need to Know I Learned in Kindergarten*. In the following excerpt, Fulghum ponders on what he would like to have for Christmas.

It's harder to talk about, but what I really, really, really want for Christmas is just this:

I want to be five years old again for an hour.
I want to laugh a lot and cry a lot.
I want to be picked up and rocked to sleep in
someone's arms, and carried up to bed just one
more time.
I know what I really want for Christmas.
I want my Childhood back.

As much as we would like it, we cannot have our childhood back. Yet in remembering the child within each of us, we can choose to give the special moments of childhood to our children, not just on Christmas morning, but every day of the year. So greet your children with extra care. Make this effort even if you're dog-tired. The nose prints on the glass will be well worth it. If necessary, practice and visualize your entrance. Practice does make perfect!

Your children need your presence
more than your presents.

—Jesse Jackson

69

Your Children Have Three Primary Emotional Needs—Meet Them

All human beings need other human beings. And we all have three basic emotional needs. Firstly, we all need to be loved. Secondly, we all need to love. The third emotional need we all share is the need to feel valued. Without the sense that we're worthwhile human beings, depression, despair, and rebellion are the likely result.

Clearly, as parents we're in a very strong position to ensure that these needs will always be fulfilled for our children. Let them know daily that they are valued and unconditionally loved because they, like you, are a child of the Creator. If you never forget their basic innocence, they'll never forget how to love, and they'll maintain their natural sense of worthiness forever.

Finally, practice *receiving* your child's love. Children don't love us on our schedule, or in the ways that we as adults prefer to express our love. Show delight over the $2.95 birthday gift that your ten-year-old buys—even though it's a pair of cuff links you never dreamed you would ever own. Recognize that your toddler's attempts to fix a flat are not his intentional efforts to frustrate you even further. Children often express their love through acts of service and truly want to help. And as you're cleaning up the flour from the floor and every nook and cranny in the kitchen, remember the love that went into baking that special cake. Learn your child's language of love and receive it. In this case, receiving is giving!

When everything is said and done, only love will last.

—The Bible

70

Each Month Make A List Of Everything You Are Grateful For Regarding Your Children And Your Life

I suggest that you make the first list today. When you're done, share it with your family. Let them see the list, which will likely include your gratitude to God for providing you with your family. Encourage them to make a list of all the things they're grateful for in their lives. Provide your children with some starter examples. Finally, have the entire family sit down and create a collective list together.

Shifting the perspective from "what's wrong?" to gratitude can have an uplifting effect on the entire family and also demonstrate to your children the value you have for them in your heart. It's an opportunity to focus on what you have instead of what you want to have.

It's not about having more, or having less. It's about having each other and really having what you have.

71

Save Yourself The Headache Of Trying To Force Your Kids To Eat Fruits, Vegetables, Liver, And Tofu

Our son taught us a lot about food. When someone tells you what you must eat, you don't eat it! And to make matters even worse, you prove that you can survive twenty-one years—even be quite healthy—without eating it. There goes another rigid belief down the tubes!

A tremendous amount of friction occurs in many families regarding the children's eating habits. Our rigid insistence that our children "eat their vegetables, clean their plates, at least try the tofu ... and hold off on dessert until every bit of liver is eaten" is counterproductive in the long-run. My experience is that these commands ruin the appetite of every family member and make the evening meal an aversive time, rather than a time of sharing, joy, and meaningful conversation.

The truth of the matter is that children do reasonably well on what appears to us adults to be a poor diet. So we must lighten up, try not to force-feed them what the latest nutrition magazine recommends, and let eating be a joyous occasion. They'll somehow get all the nourishment they need on their own, and you'll have eliminated a major source of disharmony.

There's only one hunger—the hunger for wholeness, truth, good and God.

—Bryon Katie Rolle

72

Magnificent Consequences

- What your children see you do, they will also do.
- What they do will eventually become an ingrained habit.
- The ingrained habits they develop are who they fundamentally are.
- Who they fundamentally are has consequences for the world.

Let your children see you behave lovingly and with kindness and compassion for all living things—large and small. This is a beautiful habit for them to acquire, and the consequences are magnificent.

It's within this context that the parenting process can become such a potent vehicle for the promotion of spirituality for both parent and child. Make no mistake: parenting is a spiritual call that must be heard. Have you the ears to hear?

If you sow a thought you reap an act;
If you sow an act you reap a habit;
If you sow a habit you reap a character;
If you sow a character you reap a destiny.

—Buddist Proverb

73

High EQ People Are Aware Of Their Act— Make Your Children Aware Of Theirs

No matter how perfectly you parent your children they will develop an ACT. Everybody in the whole wide world has an ACT. Shakespeare knew this—which is why he called the whole world a stage. High EQ parents are aware of their own act and help their children become aware of the act they've adopted. The task of the parent is to consistently let the children know that they are not their act. So, with your assistance, your children can get their act together. This doesn't mean they won't have an act; it means that they'll be aware of it, will have some choice about playing it, and will more or less be in charge of their act rather that it being in charge of them.

Because of how the brains of human beings are wired up, we lay down memory traces of significant events that we believe are related to our physical and psychological survival. Once we've established that a certain behavioral pattern has allowed us to psychologically or physically survive, we *automatically* play the record button for our act any time we think a threat to our survival exists. Unfortunately, by the age of twelve to fifteen, most children have come to believe that their survival is constantly at stake and are therefore practicing their act over and over again on a regular basis. Adults should not forget their own teen years, when a small slight by a member of the "in crowd" was a devastating event and most definitely was viewed as a survival issue.

The act I developed as a kid was the Tough Guy Act. When I was in the sixth grade, a group of kids made me give them my lunch money on a daily basis. They said I was buying insurance that would protect me from getting beat up. Even though I paid the "insurance" regularly, there was always a lot of pushing, shoving, and threats. I lived in constant terror. And like most other males, even after forty years I can still clearly remember the faces of the bullies who terrorized me. One day my fear became so great that I decided to "go crazy" the next time I was approached for my lunch money. The next day, when the bullies accosted me in the bathroom, I began to scream and yell. At the top of my lungs I told them I was going to kill them all, that I was prepared to fight until I was dead, and that they would never ever touch any of my money again. To my great surprise my act worked. They appeared to be afraid of me, and then, one by one, left the area with fear in their eyes. I can't recall ever having had such a sense of triumph and relief. My Tough Guy Act had worked. Unfortunately, it was so rapidly associated with survival that my brain immediately forgot that it was a contrived act. As such, it inlaid such a strong stimulus-response reaction that I automatically played my Tough Guy Act whenever I perceived a threat. And I felt threatened a lot. The result was that I played my tough guy role when it was totally inappropriate and uncalled for. The fact is, I probably never really needed it again, but, nevertheless, it came out automatically over and over again.

With insight, awareness, and practice I've come to exert a great deal of control over my act. When I feel myself slipping (automatically) into it, I can now stop the show before it becomes center stage.

Tough Guy is just one of many possible acts that can be adopted. Show-Off, Mr. Cool, Genius, Bitch, Nice Guy, Spiritual Guru, and Idiot are just a few of the many popular acts. Again, the issue is not whether you will have an act or not. The issue is whether you'll be aware of what act you've adopted. Without awareness, it will control you. With awareness, you can control it.

Anybody who knows you well can tell you what your act is. The interesting nature of acts is that everybody knows when you're in it except you.

Help your children become aware of their act. Most importantly, let them know that their act is not who they fundamentally are. When people say "I just want to be me," they're really saying

"I'm sick of my act." They've lost sight of the Sunlight of the Spirit, and that is who we all really are—a child of God whose innermost core, whose innermost essence is love.

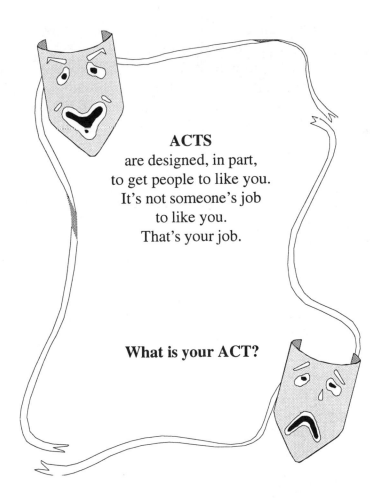

ACTS
are designed, in part,
to get people to like you.
It's not someone's job
to like you.
That's your job.

What is your ACT?

74

Teach Your Children To Get Value From All Of Life's Experiences

Many things happen that we have no control over. However, we're responsible for our experience of everything that happens. If Life presents us with difficult situations, as it often will, it's our task to learn the lessons inherent in the situation and to derive value from it. Getting value and learning lessons from Life's events is not mandatory; it's a choice that must consciously be made. Teach your children to be responsible for, and aware of, the choices they make. After twenty years of working with prison inmates, it's very clear to me that those inmates who get value from their prison time very rarely return to prison. Life gave them lessons, they learned the lessons, and they moved on. For those inmates who didn't get value from their prison experience, Life usually required that they come back for another round—for another opportunity to learn the lesson. Interestingly, the more someone hated his prison time, the more likely he was to return. For those who didn't really mind their experience, there was much less likelihood of return because they recognized the need to get value from their time.

As I mentioned earlier, Life is a master teacher. Life knows what courses we need to graduate to the next spiritual level and will keep giving us the same homework until we understand the lesson completely. The curriculum is mandatory for us all. *When* we actually graduate is our choice. We will all, every single one of us, graduate with honors—eventually. It will take some of us a very, very long time to graduate. Some of us will graduate very quickly, perhaps even in this lifetime.

The concept of "old souls" exists in some religious traditions. Allegedly, these individuals have been on the wheel of Life over the course of many lifetimes. Certainly, this concept has some level of face validity insofar as some people do appear to be much more spiritually advanced than others. My own level of spirituality is still embryonic. Despite the fact that my parents were basically loving and non-abusive, I grew up quite selfish and inconsiderate. Empathy was foreign to me until my mid-thirties. I thought it was a dangerous world and that people were inherently bad and out to get you, rather than inherently good and willing to assist you. I no longer view the world in those terms, yet I am hardly an "old soul" who came into the world with a strong spiritual outlook. I'm more of a "new soul" who has progressed some during this lifetime; but my spirituality has not yet settled deeply into my bones. In contrast, there are those whose spiritual perspective appears absolutely fundamental to their nature. In part, I'm writing this book with the hope that what I say will sink deeper into my bones. I do believe we never say anything we do not need to hear. I hope I can listen to the sound of my own voice and walk the walk, not just talk the talk. I'll need God's grace and would appreciate your blessings.

Make it thy business to know thyself, which is the most difficult lesson in the world.

—Miguel de Cervantes

75

Arguments

More needs to be said about the problem of argumentation. Arguments can steal the lifeblood of a parent-child relationship, and they can swiftly become the rule rather than the exception. Over and over again, I see relationships in which both the parent and the child have given up. They've simply checked out of the relationship. If the child is in his teen years he often checks out physically—he leaves through the front door or the back door, but he's gone. In other instances the child checks out psychologically and is no less gone than if his physical body wasn't there. Parents check out too. This usually takes the form of constant nagging, with interactions being almost solely limited to trying to change the child by criticism. This type of relationship gives a whole new meaning to the term "living hell."

I want to clearly state that you can have a relationship without any argumentation. You simply do not have to argue. Nothing in God's Universe promotes argumentation. It's also important to recognize that winning an argument is not in any way conducive to a better relationship. Arguing serves no valid purpose; it doesn't work for the betterment of the relationship; and if you choose not to participate in the argument, there won't be one because it takes two to tangle.

Every year thousands of young people are killed by a variety of means. If a tragic accident happened to one of your children, how important would all of these arguments about better grades, shorter hairstyles, cleaner rooms, or neater clothes really be then? Let's never forget what is really crucial to the parent-child relationship and never lose sight of that which is paramount. Nothing, absolutely nothing, is worth jeopardizing the loving nature of your relationship!

It helps to discuss the dynamics of argumentation with your children and spouse. Let them know that the intentions that result in argumentation involve domination and in making the other person wrong or guilty. Communication, which is the opposite of argumentation, results from the intention to have a satisfying and loving relationship no matter whether the topic is drug abuse or severe delinquency. It's that simple!

Tell your children and spouse you commit to never arguing with them again—and don't. The trick is to be aware of your real intentions when you begin to enter into an argumentative conversation. The following four-step formula will help you be more aware. Use it in all of your relationships, and teach your children to use it as well.

Step 1.   Stop talking and pause.
Step 2.   Ask yourself, "What am I trying to achieve in this conversation—to dominate or to enhance the relationship?"
Step 3.   Ask yourself, "How is what I'm doing right now preventing me from getting what I really want?"
Step 4.   Honestly state your intention to your loved one, and move on.

No fight: No blame.

—Lao Tzu,
Tao Te Ching

76

Let Your Children Know They Will Not Be Punished *For* Their Transgressions

In the divine scheme of Life, we are not punished *for* our transgressions—we are punished *by* them.

Hatred is its own punishment. The upset, anger, and mental turmoil that accompany violence are punishment. The guilt that follows is additional pain. Jealousy creates what it hopes to avoid. Jealousy, while being a painful experience in and of itself, eventually brings with it that which is most feared: the loss of the loved object. If lying is habitual, people avoid you. If you consistently try to impress people, they will be very unimpressed. Anger begets anger; unkindness brings unkindness; if you steal you'll be stolen from; if you don't treat people fairly you'll be dealt with in like kind.

A friend of mine once presented me with a hypothetical dilemma. He told me that I must choose between being a rapist or a rapee. I was stunned by the options. My initial response was an inclination to avoid being the rapee and choose being the rapist. Yet almost immediately, I experienced the intensity of anger, guilt, hatred, self-hatred, and lack of empathy it must take to be a rapist. It became clear to me that, given who I am, being a rapist would involve a great deal of pain. Harming another in this manner would be a tremendous punishment. It is a punishment for us all, whether or not we recognize it. The consequences levied out by Man are insignificant compared to the consequences imposed by the Universe. Some of us are ready to notice and others are not yet able to see.

Teach your children the principle that we're punished more *by* our transgressions than *for* them. Use every opportunity to help them incorporate this principle into their daily lives. Once this fundamental principle of Life is understood, they will naturally behave in ways that are consistent with the flow of the Universe. Let them know that God is not the big scorekeeper in the sky who will eventually punish us for the transgressions we commit. We need not fear such retaliation, and we need not fear God in any way. The commandments of Life are rarely adhered to out of fear. Instead, they are embraced because they allow for a life of peace and serenity. It is only for this reason that people choose to live in harmony with Universal law.

The following poem by Walt Whitman is a beautiful reminder of this principle:

A Song of the Rolling Earth (A Carol of Words)

Each man to himself, and each woman to herself,
    such is the work of the past and present, and the
    word of immortality;
No one can acquire for another—not one!
No one can grow for another—not one!
The song is to the singer, and comes back most to
    him;
The teaching is to the teacher, and comes back most
    to him;
The murder is to the murderer, and comes back most
    to him;
The theft is to the thief, and comes back most to him;
The love is to the lover, and comes back most to him;
The gift is to the giver, and comes back most to
    him—it cannot fail;
The oration is to the orator, the acting is to the actor
    and actress, not to the audience.
And no man understands any greatness or goodness
    but his own, or the indication of his own.

I am the suffering that I do. Suffering is optional.
— Byron Katie Rolle

77

It's Not Our Mistakes That Cause Us Problems—It's The Resistance To Admitting Them

People make too much of mistakes. Each of us is a "work in progress" that will eventually make it, and is loved in spite of our mistakes. However, most of us get caught up in the drama of our mistakes. We either dwell on them incessantly or justify them. While justification has the short-term payoff of releasing us from guilt or remorse, it is tremendously costly in the long-term. Justification simply guarantees that the same behavior will be repeated over and over. The result is a downward cycle of mistakes followed by increasingly uncomfortable consequences. Of course, we can also justify the consequences by seeing ourselves as victims—which then results in even greater mistakes and disharmony in our lives.

Teach children early to avoid justifying their mistakes. Don't ask them why they did what they did, or prod them for excuses until you receive one you'll accept. Instead, ask them about the consequences of their behavior, the effects on other people, what they've learned about their behavior, and how they intend to handle this situation if it should occur in the future. Discuss their purposes and goals, and point out how their behavior is incongruent with them. Remind them that their choice is between denying or defending a behavior that brings disharmony, or simply admitting that what they did was an error and moving on. The best way for them to learn this is for them to witness us doing it with them when we make mistakes.

You can readily assess a person's level of EQ by looking at their willingness to learn from their mistakes. When Thomas

Edison invented the light bulb, he tried over two thousand experiments before he got it to work. A young reporter asked him how it felt to fail so many times. Edison responded, "I never failed once. I invented the light bulb. It just happened to be a two-thousand-step process." High EQ people are not perfect people. High EQ people are people who correct their mistakes and move on— no matter how many times it takes!

Do your child a great service. If every time he makes a mistake you lovingly ask, "What have you learned from this error?", you'll be doing your child a valuable service. If every time you make a mistake you lovingly ask, "What have I learned from this error?", you'll be doing your child a great service. Share what you've learned from your mistakes with your child.

Owning up to mistakes seems almost impossible at first. Most of us are initially like the caterpillar that looked at the butterfly in flight and said, "You'll never get me up in one of those things."

78

Let Your Children Know Why God Made Them

An old Sufi story—

Past the seeker as he prayed came the crippled and the beggar and the beaten. And seeing them the holy one went down into deep prayer and cried, "Great God, how is it that a loving creator can see such things and yet do nothing about them?" And out of a long silence, God said, "I did do something. I made you."

Almost every single one of us has the feeling that we are not really loveable, not really important. We must always try to remember that these feelings are totally false. Let's also remember that we do make a difference, that we are magnificent, beautiful, and deeply loved by our Creator.

Your job as a parent is to remind your children why God made them. You must touch them so deeply that you uncap the spirit in their soul. Only your love can do this.

We all need to be touched in the deepest part of our lives, to have our spirit uncapped. If you uncap it, it will go everywhere. That is why we're here.

—Reverend Cecil Williams

79

If I Could Do It All Again

Most of us learn to be parents by making mistakes. It is in the process of parenting that we learn what is really important. So often we look back at our mistakes with regrets, wishing we could have another chance. Since life doesn't give us another chance, it is up to us to make peace with our mistakes and to recognize them as important life lessons that can be passed on to our grown children or to others.

I have taken a step in this direction by writing the following poem. It was written shortly before my son's 21st birthday.

IF I COULD DO IT ALL AGAIN

If I could do it all again—

I'd focus more on quality—and less on quantity.

I'd pay less attention to perfection—and more on making a loving connection.

I'd encourage him to dream more, and stress the middle class dream less.

I'd pay more attention to increasing the size of his heart—and less on increasing the size of our bank account.

I'd care for him even more—and worry less about giving him more.

I'd live each day like it was our last—and make plans as if we were to live forever.

I'd specify certain conditions—and my love would be unconditional.

I'd forever recognize that play was not work—

And above all else I would make every interaction an opportunity to share kindness, love and joy.

80

Take Temperament Into Consideration

Temperament is our genetic endowment that tends to predispose us to certain moods and behavioral displays. If you have more than one child, the chances are that you've noticed some significant differences between them. Research continues to indicate that children have an inborn tendency towards shyness, boldness, cheerfulness, or a depressed mood. These tendencies are allegedly the result of different patterns of brain activity. This isn't very good news for those of us who enter the world with a tendency towards shyness or depression, or who have children with these inclinations.

However, research has also shown that parents can help their children to cope with shyness and fearfulness. In Daniel Goleman's book entitled *Emotional Intelligence,* he devotes an entire chapter to "Temperament Is Not Destiny." In this chapter Goleman suggests parenting techniques that can assist your children to adapt to their natural temperament. I continue to strongly recommend this book as mandatory reading for anyone truly interested in a thorough explanation of Emotional Intelligence.

Parents can also do a great deal to curb any inclinations towards delinquency. A growing body of research suggests a connection between violence and certain types of brain chemistry. Most important, though, is the suggestion that it frequently takes a history of trauma to stimulate the aggression and violence that perhaps would otherwise lie dormant. My experience as a prison psychologist for over twenty years indicates that a significant majority of inmates were the victims of either sexual, physical, or verbal abuse over a long period of time by adults who were often their parental figures or relatives. As a parent, keep in mind that consistent verbal abuse may be as damaging as physical or perhaps even sexual abuse. It is vital that we make the commitment to avoid abusive behavior of any kind and take steps to protect our children from it. Abuse clearly has long-term negative ramifications for the child's EQ. If you have concerns about child abuse, seek professional help or contact Parents Anonymous in your community.

The best things you can give children, next to good habits, are good memories.

—Sydney J. Harris

81

Depression In Pre-Teens And Teenagers

Depression among the young has increased dramatically in recent years. Research suggests that early depressive episodes are often predictors of later more severe depression.

As parents, we can promote a world view that can inhibit the development of depression in our children. Developing good relationship skills early in the home is a vital key to avoiding depression. Much of what children get depressed about are the relationship problems that exist with the parents. If the parents can remain aware of the fact that the most fundamental issue within the parent-child relationship is love, it's unlikely that relationship problems will develop.

As mentioned earlier, whether we're arguing or communicating is strictly dependent upon our intentions. If the intention is to make someone wrong, yourself right, or to dominate the other person, you don't have communication, but rather argumentation.

In addition to promoting positive relationship skills, it's important to be aware of depression-promoting thought patterns that can develop in response to negative events that are virtually inevitable: breaking up with a girlfriend or boyfriend, being rejected by a popular group, having a teacher who is biased against you, not making the cheerleading or football squad, and so forth.

As parents, it is important to intervene in the right way. Help your children to challenge negative thinking patterns with optimistic alternatives, and teach them or ensure that they receive assertive training skills. Dr. Albert Ellis has numerous books in print that are designed to change negative self-talk. Good assertive training skills classes and books are widely available. I recommend both before depression becomes an issue.

Most importantly, recognize that your capicity to help your children when that are in need depends upon the state of your own mind. As human beings we do not have a choice about whether we will think or not. The choice we have is what we will think. And this choice has a tremendous impact on the quality of our lives.

For someone deeply trapped in a prison of thought, how good it can feel to meet a mind that hears, a heart that reassures. It's as if a listening mind is, in and of itself, an invitation to another mind to listen too. How much it can mean when we accept the invitation and hear the world anew.

—Ram Dass & Paul Gorman
How Can I Help?

I wanted to end my life at 14 years old.
I've had the feeling for 10 years.
Now—after reading your books—
I promise myself to never feel that way again.

—Anonymous,
Chicken Soup for the Christian Soul

82

Returning The Gift—
We Must Give Back To Receive Again

High EQ parents recognize that their children are gifts. They further recognize that the time comes when we must let our children go. Clutching them to our breast for too long hinders their growth and ours. When this time comes, we'll recognize it, for it is clearly stated in the eyes of the child.

Paradoxically, if we surrender, bless them on their way, and give them back to God—we can have them forever. If we can't let them go we can't have them, for the Universe won't allow us to have that which we are not willing to give away. Have your children forever; let them go when the time comes.

Complete possession is proved only by giving. All you are unable to give possesses you.

—Andre Gide

83

What We Don't Pass On To Our Children Is Vital To Them

What most of us consider to be the most important things to leave our children involve financial security. We would like them to have property, money, possessions, and position in society. With this in mind, many parents become quite anxious about their own financial situation and hope in some way to be able to contribute to the future security of their children. Tremendous emphasis is placed on education as a means to success in life. As the children enter their teen years, increasing pressure, future concerns, and a sense of urgency replace much of the former atmosphere of love with a sense of anxiety. The parents' anxiety is cast out onto the children, who eventually incorporate it as their own. Love and anxiety are not very compatible; consequently, survival concerns begin to dominate the relationship and love becomes second fiddle. The child is often bombarded with "What are you going to do with yourself if you don't go to college? You don't want to work like a slave for peanuts. Times are hard and you need to decide a lot of important things early in life."

All this pressure might be justified if financial security and having the "American Dream" were related to peace and tranquility. It is important that we not fall prey to the anxiety concerns that are promoted by our materialistic and prestige-oriented society.

The real issue is for parents to raise a child with a high EQ. Such children will recognize that inner peace is more valuable than possessions and finances. And if possessions and finances do come their way, they'll know how to enjoy them and use them wisely. These children will exhibit the justice, love, sense of fairness, empathy, obligation to others, and God orientation that will bring them spiritual harmony and a healthy sense of responsibility and compassion. Don't dull the twinkle of a star by imposing upon them a way of life based upon the acquisition of external commodities, at the expense of developing the internal values that lead to an abiding peace.

The ideals which have lighted my way, and time after time have given me new courage to face life cheerfully, have been kindness, beauty, and truth... The trite subjects of human efforts—possessions, outward success, luxury—have always seemed to me contemptible.

—Albert Einstein

84

Why Did You Become A Parent?

Most of us have never really asked ourselves this question. Sometimes the motivation is to revive a marriage, or to fulfill what may be deemed a societal obligation or a feminine/masculine role. Sometimes even the most positive of motivations can have a selfish side to them and, to whatever extent that may be true, our children are a disappointment to us.

Carl Jung once said, "Nothing has a stronger influence psychologically on their environment and especially on their children than the unlived life of the parent." What Jung was referring to is the unspoken expectation that our children will complete us in some way—do for us what we couldn't do for ourselves. From this perspective, a child becomes an extension of the parent. And each of the child's "shortcomings" is accompanied by a sense of betrayal or personal failure that often comes to a head during the teenage years.

It is virtually impossible for any child to satisfy all the ego desires of even a reasonable set of parents. Parenting must be as free as possible from selfish desires to ensure that the parent-child relationship doesn't become about enhancing the parents' self-esteem. Our children are not here to make us look good in the eyes of other people. When such factors creep into the relationship, turmoil, judging, rejection, and emotional entanglement begin to characterize the relationship. Strong expectations are potential disaster, for every child comes into the world with a unique temperament and will definitely develop a mind of his own to some degree. Set your ego expectations aside and bless your children as they go along the path they've chosen. They're going to go that way whether you bless them or not; so bless them, love them, accept who they are even if they don't meet your ideal. If you do this, they will love you and be your friend, both now and in your old age. Once again, we must surrender in order to win.

Allow children to be happy in their own way,
for what better way will they ever find?

—Dr. Johnson,
Chop Wood, Carry Water

It is vital that we choose
our children exactly the
way they are—
and, exactly the way
they are not!

85

How Would You Have Liked To Have Been Treated As A Child?

When your child was born you obviously became a parent. It's one of those rare things that happen suddenly—one day you aren't a parent, and the next day you are. I can think of very few other changes in life that are so sudden and transformational. So it's not as if we gradually became parents and had a lengthy period of opportunity to learn the ropes prior to the bundle of joy's arrival. We can read child-rearing books—but this is knowledge, not wisdom.

Yet we've all had a history of being a child, and when we become parents we can all ask, "What would an ideal parent have been?" What did we not receive as a child that we really needed? How could we have been treated so that we would have become better human beings? What mistakes did our parents make? If we don't look hard at these issues, it's very likely that we will parent our children in very much the same way we were parented. Is that good news?

Our parenting affords us the opportunity to rectify the mistakes of the past and to ensure that our children receive the things that we may have failed to receive when we were children. It's often said that not one of us, not one, has received enough love. It is awareness of this truism that can rectify the problem and break the cycle of poor parenting. It is vitally important that we treat our children the way we would have liked to be treated as a child—treated in a way that would make every child a fully functioning human being.

Our children give us the opportunity to become
the parent we always wish we had.

—Nancy Samalin

86

Teach Your Children To Watch Their Minds

My wife often tells a story about an outing that she and my son made when he was only five years old. She had decided to take him to the movies to see a cartoon. Since we were new to the Austin area she was unsure of exactly where the theatre was located. She ended up going to the wrong theatre and driving madly through town to get to the right one before the movie started. At one point she came to a congested intersection that was under construction. Just as she missed the green light she began to lose it—yelling at another driver, which was very uncharacteristic of her. At that moment my son looked up at her and, with his five-year-old wisdom, simply stated, "Mom, you're not watching your mind." To say the least, my wife was caught off guard. Her intention was to show my son a good time. Yet something had got in the way, and it took a five-year-old to recognize it. Yes, it was her mind!

How often does the average parent start out with good intentions and then end up with a mess because either he or his child forgot to watch his mind? I believe it happens all the time. I heard one adult admit that when he was between the ages of twelve and seventeen, he and his father did not exchange one word, even though they lived under the same roof. Can you imagine the disease in a household like that? What could possibly be on their minds? While this is indeed an extreme example, I believe it isn't much more damaging than most of the communication between many teenagers and their parents.

Vigilantly watch your mind, and teach your child to do the same. The mind is instinctive. Its purpose is to survive. Its job is to search for danger. It is very similar to a bouncer at a local bar: it has very little insight, is always looking for trouble, and is totally convinced it is "right". Consequently, it creates a lot of problems when no one is looking. It definitely needs watching.

It will be helpful if you and your child recognize that you are not your mind, but something greater. The mind is a tool. It is to be used, and used effectively. Begin to ask your mind questions and insist on the truth. One very important question is this: "Is anything at all worth the pain of separation from what is potentially the most gratifying relationship in life?" Anybody in his right mind would answer, "No, absolutely not."

Also, parents must remember that their teenage children are usually not rebelling against them, but against the inflexibility of their demands for a certain type of behavior. The behavior in question would very likely fall by the wayside as the child grows older anyway. How many teens of the 1960's still have shoulder-length hair and flowers behind their ear? Relax. With some problems, you don't need to change anything—except your mind!

To stay in the experience of loving a person requires accurate and vigilant observation of the mind. Otherwise you become unconscious, treat others with automaticity and love dies for lack of your participation... Only you have the power to observe. You cannot depend on your mind to do it for you since it is not in the scope of the mind's power to observe itself.

—Ron Smothermon, M.D.

87

Parenting Provides The Optimum
Opportunity To Grow Spiritually

I really don't think it is possible to have created a better learning and growth environment than the one this world provides. And when you add the task of parenting to the whole picture, the learning possibilities explode. There seems to be a new lesson around every corner if we're willing to be open and learn. Along with this vast smorgasbord of lessons come both pleasure and pain. And it's the painful lessons that offer the greatest opportunities for change.

One of the most difficult changes for most parents to make is to give up child-rearing practices that simply do not work. We all have a set of conscious and unconscious strategies. If nothing else, we unconsciously repeat what we learned from our parents, even if we were very dissatisfied with their techniques. It's not like we try them, discover they are ineffective to use with our own children, and then give them up. What happens is that we apply them, they don't work, and we continue to apply them (usually forever) with the determination to make them work. We do this because we think our techniques are right and, in part, because it's the only game we really know how to play.

A more "seemingly" advanced strategy is to consult a host of popular child-rearing books and to apply the techniques these books offer with respect to specific problems. I don't know of anyone who does this successfully. Professors in my graduate psychology department used to claim that psychological techniques would work on everyone except your own child.

If techniques don't work, what does? When your purpose is to have a spiritual and loving relationship with your children you will have one, and your parent-child relationship will be magical.

This is the universal technique that will work if it is used as the foundation of all other techniques. The irony is that all techniques work when love is present and domination is absent. Unfortunately, domination is usually present and love is often absent, even though we don't recognize it and steadfastly proclaim our loving motivation. But, once again, most of us would be embarrassed by what a videotape of our interactions with our children would show.

Each problem or issue that is handled in this loving-spiritual framework will be a springboard to your growth, your child's growth, and will enhance the entire family's relationship. This requires persistent effort—reflecting on your own character and motives, thinking through problems, and making decisions that promote the spiritual growth of both your children and yourselves. There is simply no quick-fix advice or solution that will make you an effective parent without going through the time and effort to be one.

When you forget and try to apply some sensible-sounding technique without your spirit up front, the results won't be sensible and the relationship will fail to grow. The lesson to be learned will be provided again and again until you properly learn it. (Isn't it interesting how often the same issues keep coming up time after time?) You might be able to eliminate the *symptom* of some immediate problem. Yet the underlying condition will remain, and eventually new symptoms will appear in a more serious and painful form. The more parents are into quick-fix advice, the more the child surprises them with new problems that can't be fixed with their new tried and true method.

Children are our best and most persistent spiritual teachers. They aren't easily satisfied. They're partners with the Universe and will repeat a lesson until you get it. Once you learn the lesson the Universe sees no need for further repetition and the problem disappears.

The greatest decisions of life are made daily in the silent inner garden of the soul.

—Jack Hawley, *Reawakening the Spirit in Work*

88

Teach Your Children How To Deal With Change

Children are affected by what is going on in the world, and the world is changing. Our children have to adapt to changes that have come more quickly and in larger numbers than in any other time in history—and many of those changes are simply beyond their control.

The ability to adapt to change is a major component of high EQ. It requires flexible thinking and the ability to look at situations and problems from a variety of perspectives. It requires understanding the world, as well as discovering the balance between satisfying individual needs and caring for all people and the future of our planet. Most of all, it requires a faith in oneself and the ability to deal with uncertainty with confidence and a sense of purpose.

I believe that our children's inability to deal with uncertainty and change often leaves them with a sense of being overwhelmed and the idea that nothing really makes a difference. (Hence, the current teenage jargon, "Whatever.") They are without meaning. Children without meaning have two choices. They may do what their parents tell them to do out of loyalty. Or, they may do the opposite of what their parents tell them to do with a sense of disloyalty. In the first case we have compliance, in the second noncompliance. The first is obviously better than the second. But in both cases there is no deep personal commitment!

Parents contribute to this problem. Often parents don't encourage their children to deal with change because they're unable to deal with the uncertainty of change themselves. They presume that the world is as it was when they were children and insist that their child follow in their footsteps. Most of us deny change because we doubt our ability to live with it. We then transfer these doubts to our children. The result is a lot of useless anxiety.

To deny change is like stepping out into a busy intersection in a growing town or swimming against a raging torrent—it's dangerous and it's no use! Don't deny it. Instead, teach your children basic principles that will assist them in dealing with a changing world. You might find that they not only make it unscathed, but also that they become instruments of change themselves. Many aspects of life today need to be changed—pollution, war, and hunger, to name a few. No doubt, high EQ children will be our future leaders.

Don't limit a child to your own learning, for he was born in another time.

—Rabbinic saying

The art of living... is neither careless drifting on the one hand nor fearful clinging to the past and the known on the other. It consists in being completely sensitive to each moment, in regarding it utterly new and unique, in having the mind open and wholly receptive.

—Alan W. Watts,
The Wisdom of Insecurity

89

Time Is Love To Children

Children want a lot of our time, and many parents simply don't provide it. Young children who aren't given meaningful interaction time often isolate themselves from their parents as they grow older. To children, time is love. As they get older and approach their teenage years, they naturally require and want less of our time and attention. They enter school, acquire friends, and spend less time at home. Nevertheless, when they are older and do require our attention, it's usually for a very important reason. Be sensitive to these subtle times.

If you don't provide loving attention to them when they're young, they will likely go elsewhere with their problems when these important issues do arise. It isn't easy to give freely of our time in this society, even for the most loving and responsible of parents. In a single-parent home or a home with two working parents, time and energy are often at a premium. But it is vital to not simply say our children are the most important things in our lives; it is necessary to act like it. This takes sacrifice now. The old cliché that no one on his deathbed says he wishes he would have spent more time at the office or cleaning the house is true. The thing that matters during such critical times is the quality of our relationships—did we love fully and well; did we put the important things off for too long; did we do our best to raise children of integrity?

It's very easy to feel guilty in this area. How much time is enough time? Don't we also need some time to ourselves? There were many times I didn't play with my son, or did so resentfully. As I look back now, I wish I had never missed a single one of his requests to join him when he said, "Let's play, Dad." As I write this I am sad for each missed opportunity. Yet I know this is unrealistic. No parent has the time or true inclination to attend to every one of his child's requests in a loving way. We are hardly perfect, yet we can strive for perfection. My son, who is twenty-one now, has heard my apologies. Additionally, I've written him stories and poems expressing my regrets for my lack of perfection. They've been well-received.

Simply do the best you can in this area. But do the best you can with full recognition that our children are our highest priority in life.

If alcohol or excessive stress is a barrier to spending time with your children, get assistance for these problems. Ten percent of the U.S. population has problems with alcohol. The average problem drinker spends approximately twelve hours per week drinking. This is a tremendous amount of valuable time lost, which could be spent raising the EQ level of our children.

Spending time with our children is our sacred duty.

Dost thou love life? Then do not squander time;
for that's the stuff life is made of.

—Benjamin Franklin

90

When Serious Problems Do Arise

By serious problems I don't mean getting C's in school instead of A's and B's. Nor do I mean finding *Playboy* under the mattress, or occasional bursts of anger. By serious problems I mean drug abuse, juvenile delinquency, gang involvement, episodes of cruelty to people or animals, or regular violent outbursts.

When such problems do occur, parents desperately want answers to these specific issues and often expect, or at least hope, that cookbook-type answers exist somewhere. My experience indicates that techniques and procedures for dealing with these issues really don't exist. You can certainly find many books that give you a host of seemingly plausible suggestions to implement when your child becomes uncontrollable, but rarely do they prove to be effective. Our approach involves the belief that it's not the problem-solving strategy that is used, but the attitude that the parents bring to the situation. An ancient Eastern saint told us, "Do whatever you must with a person, but never put him out of your heart."

How often it is that we put our children out of our hearts when they bring shame and embarrassment into our lives. During the times when we lose our temper, yell, scream, and threaten, we have literally stopped loving them. When anger and judgment are present, love is absent. We must never stop loving our children and never lose sight of that part of them that is spiritual. We must maintain our commitment to holding this vision even when that spiritual spark isn't evident to them or to us. After over twenty years of full-time prison work as a psychologist in three major United States penitentiaries, I can promise you that the spiritual spark is never completely extinguished. So we must maintain our commitment to our children, and commitment means—no matter what! No matter what happens or how they behave we must be there with unconditional love and never put them out of our hearts, even if we must put them out of our lives.

During these times of crisis it is recommended that you voice your commitment to them, and most importantly that you demonstrate it to them. You may have to go beyond your feelings to do this, but this effort will bear fruit even though it may not be immediately evident. They'll eventually come to see in themselves what it is you see in them. It's often easy for us parents to look into the crib of our three-month-old child and feel assured that he is indeed a child of God. It's considerably more difficult to look at our nineteen-year-old child and recognize they are the same child of God they always were. It is our responsibility to maintain that vision; the quality of the child's life may hang in the balance. Indeed, the quality of a great many people's lives hangs in the balance.

Your job on Earth, therefore, is not to learn (because you already know), but to re-member who you are. And to re-member who everyone else is. That is why a big part of your job is to remind others (that is, to re-mind) so that they can re-member also. All the wonderful teachers have been doing just that. It is your sole purpose. That is to say your soul purpose.

—Neale Donald Walsh,
Conversations with God

91

Parenting Will Bring With It A Whole New Meaning To The Word *Love*— And A Whole New Meaning To The Word *Worry*

The nature of the world is that the more we care for and love something or someone, the more we fear the loss of the loved object. We don't seem to be able to have our cake and eat it too. We are like the bee that gets stuck in its own sweet honey. As a parent, the love you will experience for your children will be rivaled by no other experience. It is qualitatively and quantitatively different than any other sensation. So it is that parenting brings with it a whole new meaning to the word *love*. In similar fashion, we won't know the real depths of worry until we face the real and imagined concerns we have about our children. I don't think there's any way of avoiding this dualistic experience— it's simply part and parcel of being a good parent and good human being. It is a cross we must bear. Yet it helps us to recognize that we, the concerned parents, often experience more difficulty than the children we're so worried about. I suspect that some of this is due to our genetic inclinations regarding our children. It may be that we're simply biologically programmed to worry about our children's survival. I do know that high EQ people recognize this dualistic nature of parenting and accept the secondary concerns of worry and anxiety as a necessary part of experiencing the greatest joys that God offers His creations.

> The love we experience is the doughnut, while the worry we experience is the hole. Keep your focus on the doughnut.

92

Beware Of Laziness

The greatest barrier to good physical health is laziness. The greatest barrier to good psychological health is laziness. The greatest barrier to intellectual growth is laziness. The greatest barrier to spiritual growth is laziness. The greatest barrier to high Emotional Intelligence is laziness. Beware of laziness!

It takes a lot of effort to overcome our laziness. Playing games with a six-year-old can be quite boring and a drain on our energy. Loving our children takes work. Often our love is just there, while at other times we must choose it. It therefore requires that we sometimes must go beyond how we feel. In a very real sense, our love is most powerfully demonstrated when we behave lovingly, even though we don't feel like it at the time.

Most people have heard that consistency is the basis of effective parenting. Parents who love their children only when they feel like it give what I call "random love." Random love is love that comes depending upon the unpredictable moods and feelings of the parent. It is inconsistent, has little or no relationship to the child, and always seems to be in too short a supply.

The opposite of random love is "unconditional love." Unconditional love doesn't mean being a push-over no matter what our children do. Unconditional love is having the *discipline* as parents to put love in the forefront of whatever we must do to help our children grow—whether it's praising them or confronting them about their misbehavior. It isn't based on our moods (random love) or whether our child's behavior makes us look good (conditional love). It is love based on an appreciation of the spirit of the child and an unmoving commitment to make that spirit all that it can be.

Extension of ourselves or moving out against inertia we call work. Moving out in the face of fear we call courage. Love, then, is a form of work or courage. Specifically, it is the work or courage directed toward the nurture of our own or another's spiritual growth.

—M. Scott Peck,
The Road Less Traveled

93

Paradoxically, We Can Only Recognize That We Are Somebody Special, When We Know That We Are Not

Clearly, the least impressive of us is often the one who is trying to be the most impressive. The show usually comes off poorly and the actor is frequently unaware that the audience sees through the charade. A long-time inmate once told me, "I've spent my whole life trying to be cool and everybody knew I wasn't. Now I don't care much about being cool and most everybody thinks I am."

My response to this man, whom I admired and thought was very cool, was this: "Before you truly understood that you were nobody special, you thought you were somebody special and you tried very hard to prove it to the world—and the world didn't recognize you. Once you truly understood that you were nobody special, you instantly became somebody special and you stopped trying to prove it to the world—and the world acknowledged you for being very special."

Mother Teresa, a great saint of our times, was often perplexed by the attention she got. She didn't see herself as anyone special.

High EQ people don't think they are anybody special—that's why they are.

In this life we cannot do great things.
We can only do small things with great love.

—Mother Teresa

168 HOW TO RAISE YOUR CHILD'S EMOTIONAL INTELLIGENCE

94

A Parent's Job

Over seven hundred years ago, Saint Francis wrote a prayer that deeply relates to what I believe the job of a parent is today. The prayer reads:

> Lord, make me a channel of thy peace—that where there is hatred, I may find love—that where there is wrong, I may find the spirit of <u>forgiveness</u>—that where there is discord, I may bring <u>harmony</u>—that where there is error, I may bring <u>truth</u>—that where there is doubt, I may bring <u>faith</u>—that where there is despair, I may bring <u>hope</u>—that where there are shadows, I may bring light—that where there is sadness, I may bring <u>joy</u>. Lord, grant that I may seek rather to <u>comfort</u> than be comforted—to <u>understand</u> rather than to be understood—to <u>love</u> than be loved. For it is by self-forgetting that one finds. It is by <u>forgiving</u> that one is forgiven. It is by dying that one awakens to Eternal Life.
> Amen.

Look at the words I've taken the liberty of underlining: forgiveness, harmony, truth, faith, hope, joy, light, comfort, understand, love, and forgiving. To bring these qualities into the life of our children is our job as parents. None of us can do so with total perfection. But we don't need to do things perfectly to raise a high EQ child; we simply need to be willing to make this work our highest priority in life. Our highest priority should be our commitment to bring forth our child's humanity—to bring forth their decency.

There is only one reason to do anything: as a statement to the universe of Who You Are. There is only one reason to un-do anything: because it is no longer a statement of Who You Want to Be.

—Neale Donald Walsh,
Conversations with God

95

Teach The Miracle

A sizeable portion of humankind's children has not been raised in a nourishing and loving environment. They don't believe they're truly loveable. Without feeling loved they can't give love, since the Universe won't allow anyone to give what they do not have.

A man whose spiritual and psychological growth has grown immensely over the last few years made the following comment: "I now know that many people love me. But them loving me is not the greatest miracle. The greatest miracle of my life is that I now am able to believe that they love me."

It is vital that we teach our children that they're loveable. Wherever your relationship with your children is, start from there and start right now. Teach the miracle!

Life is a song—sing it
Life is a game—play it
Life is a challenge—meet it
Life is a dream—realize it
Life is a sacrifice—offer it
Life is love—enjoy it.

—Sai Baba

96

Avoid Tap Dancing

There is an unhealed part in almost every single one of us that thinks we need the approval of everyone and everybody. But it's important that we let our children know that they can't tap dance fast enough, long enough, or good enough to make everybody happy. It's just not possible. What is possible is that they work at making God happy and themselves peaceful. If they're successful at making God happy and themselves peaceful, most other people will be in approval anyway.

A good start at this is to recognize what Byron Katie Rolle calls *three kinds of business*: God's business, other people's business, and our own business. We have no business in God's business. We have no business in the business of others. That leaves our own business. When we tend to just our business, it's surprising how peaceful we can be and how smoothly things can go. Model these principles for your children.

It's simply impossible to get enough attention and praise from others to make our souls content. The order of things is self-love first. Only when self-love is in place can we feel worthy of the affection of others. In the final analysis, self-love and other-love are synonymous.

97

Children As Teachers

Could it be that our children represent the single-most potent, potential teachers for us? We see our task as teaching *them* about life, but perhaps it is also their task to teach *us* about life. We don't automatically get wiser with age. Ron Smothermon, M.D., suggests, "It may be that wisdom is lost with age and that we have a lot to learn from children, not the information they have to offer, but the spirit of aliveness they have, and the absence of beliefs, and strongly held opinions."

The spirit of aliveness—that's really what we all long for, isn't it? We need to go no further than our children to find the perfect model.

Our children will show us that the spirit of aliveness is not something that can be artificially created. Notice the difference between a ten-year-old's joy in playing in the swimming pool versus his experience of being taken to the Grand Canyon by his parents to "enjoy" the experience. Children rarely react the way we want them to when we take them fishing, go to a college sporting event, visit the Washington Monument, or impose on them some event about which we have an "expectation." Our expectations are generally small catastrophes waiting to happen. From this we can learn that fun and aliveness are now, and that planning to have fun by feeling alive tomorrow usually doesn't match our expectancy.

❧

No Spirit—No Aliveness
Know Spirit—Know Aliveness

People say that what we're all seeking is a meaning for life... I think that what we're all seeking is an experience of being alive, so that our life experiences on the purely physical plane will have resonance within our innermost being and reality, so that we can actually feel the rapture of being alive.

—Joseph Campbell

98

Teach Your Children How To Solve Problems

The Bible tells us that it is better to teach a man to fish than give him a fish. Yet many parents give their child "fish" and are frustrated when, in his teenage and early adult years, he's still dependent upon them to solve life's problems.

Teach your child early how to solve problems. As you do so keep the following points in mind:

Focus on your point of leverage. When most people solve problems, they miss their greatest point of leverage. They focus on what they would *like* to change (the weaknesses of other people, or circumstances over which they have no control) and miss what can be changed. It's like the little man looking for his keys under the lamppost. When he's asked if this is where he last saw his keys, he responds, "No, but this is where the light is."

Teach your children to focus their time and energy on the things they can do something about. I've worked with hundreds of people, helping them to discover their "point of leverage" in a problem situation. Almost always the point of leverage—that place where they can make a difference—begins with themselves. Most often these problem situations involve interpersonal relationships (marriage, parents, work) in which the person has spent years trying to change the other person. Remarkably, this only happens when the individual lets go of this demand and begins to focus on himself—his perceptions, style of communicating, expectations, and skills.

Recognize that how you see a problem is the problem. Our biggest obstacle to solving most problems is how we've initially defined them. More often than not, our initial definition of the problem leads us to a quick-fix solution that leaves the real problem festering. As a society, we've done this with poverty ("give 'em welfare"), crime ("build more prisons") and drugs ("Just say No!"). But more subtle examples are evident in everyday life: Feel bad?—take a drug. Marriage problems?—get divorced. Kid problems?—kick 'em out! Teach your children to question their basic assumptions about problems and to search for long-term rather than short-term solutions.

Be creative. Most problems do not require *more* effort but *creative* effort. We generally approach problems like a fly trapped at a window. We buzz around incessantly—making a lot of noise—but get absolutely nowhere. We then react to our failure by trying a little harder. What a relief it would be if we simply turned around and looked for a different way. When faced with a problem, help your children think of at least one possible solution they haven't thought of before.

Don't make their problem your problem. When problems occur, your task as a parent is to help your children take the energy they're wasting by blaming others or making excuses, and to use it to productively explore alternative solutions. This will be difficult if you take on their problems as your own. You'll feel compelled to defend your child rather than to help him solve the problem. This is natural—after all, this is *your* child! Yet this is not only giving your child a fish, but a spoiled one. Self-pity won't serve him in the long-run, and there will be consequences. Empower your children. They aren't hopeless victims of an uncaring world.

God, give me the serenity to accept the things I cannot change, the courage to change the things I can, and the wisdom to know the difference.
Serenity Prayer,
—Alcoholics Anonymous

Self-pity in its early stage is as snug as a feather mattress. Only when it hardens does it become uncomfortable.
—Maya Angelou

99

Teach Your Children To Use Leisure Time Effectively

Most adults in our society are eager for retirement and more leisure time. Free time, long extended vacations, the opportunity to sleep in or to do absolutely nothing if we so desire, are all associated with the belief of increased happiness and less stress. These are a set of very strong assumptions that almost all of us harbor to some degree. Unfortunately, these beliefs are not consistent with research nor our own experience. The reality of too much leisure time is that it is correlated with chronic depression, anxiety, and reports of physical illness.

How can this be so? According to 20 years of research by Mihaly Csikszentmihalyi, author of *Finding Flow*, adults and children need activities which challenge them and offer the opportunity for problem solving and learning new things. Most activities which produce a strong feeling of enjoyment have clear goals, focus our attention, and make demands on our physical or mental skills. Yet, many leisure activities lack these qualities. Consequently, people often feel listless and bored when faced with free time.

Television presents a special problem, especially for our children. Children, according to Csikszentmihalyi, receive little challenge from watching television and do not report much satisfaction from doing so. Yet they clearly spend a great deal of time involved in this activity. Paradoxically, even though they report more fulfillment from participation in games and sports, they spend much less time involved in these activities and continue to stick with the less enjoyable ones. Despite the fact that "I'm bored" is something most parents hear with increasing frequency as their child gets older, the child appears unwilling to engage in activiities which they know will increase positive feelings and alleviate boredom. So it is that even though our teenagers recognize that being positively active increases their sense of well-being, they frequently opt for watching television, just hanging around, sleeping, or doing nothing.

As parents we must be aware that too much unstructured time takes away from the quality of life. Human beings must overcome an initial state of inertia and laziness to engage in productive leisure activities. Clearly, it takes more effort and energy to organize a game of basketball, than it does to sit down in front of the television. Additionally, it may take 20 to 30 minutes of being engaged in an activity before we feel more alive, challenged and energetic. If we lack the discipline to surmount these initial obstacles, our minds generally take over and offer a multitude of reasons or excuses which make it more and more difficult to move off the couch.

High EQ parents have learned how to use their leisure time effectively. They are aware of the paradox that we must expend energy in order to have more. Consequently, they are willing to experience the "negativity" that the preparation for meaningful activity generally entails. For example, they are willing to drive 30 minutes to take guitar lessons, realizing that the long term payoff will be worth the effort.

Of course, we must encourage our children to do the same. Start in their early years and frequently point out to them that many things that are ultimately enjoyable take an initial outlay of effort. Let them know that the good life is not to be found in long term idleness. We can't sleep ourselves happy nor can television fulfill the needs of the heart and soul.

So, we must model a life of activity and whenever possible take our children with us so that they too can experience the benefits of actively participating in life. We must learn to teach our children to overcome the mind's natural inclination to offer excuses and rationalizations when faced with new challenges. Do not let your child be the kind of individual who does not participate in the vast array of activities Life has to offer.

*Luckily, the world is absolutely full of interesting
things to do. Only lack of imagination, or lack of
energy, stand in the way.*

—Mihaly Csikszentmihalyi

RESOLUTIONS

People are unreasonable, illogical, and self-centered. Love them anyway.

If you do good, people may accuse you of selfish motives. Do good anyway.

If you are successful, you may win false friends and true enemies. Succeed anyway.

The good you do today may be forgotten tomorrow. Do good anyway.

Honesty and transparency make you vulnerable. Be honest and transparent anyway.

What you spend years building may be destroyed overnight. Build anyway.

People who really want help may attack you if you help them. Help them anyway.

Give the world the best you have and you may get hurt. Give the world your best anyway.

The world is full of conflict. Choose peace of mind anyway.

—Anonymous

100

Help Your Children Live Purposely

People want to matter—want for it to make a difference that they were here. Stated another way, they want to have a sense of purpose.

I believe that we all have purpose the moment we're born. This isn't a single God-given purpose that we must spend our lives trying to discover (like a treasure hunt) until we get it right. Rather, I think we all have purpose because we are given the gift of life on a planet that has a purpose—the purpose to learn, to create, and to express our God-like nature.

We are all born with unlimited potential. *How we express our purpose is the choices that we make with our life.* In a sense we are always "on purpose." If you want to know what your *true* purpose is, simply notice what has come to you in your life. Your life is the sum of all the choices you've made—even those insignificant ones you've forgotten about long ago. People get what they've chosen. Whether or not they were aware of the choice makes very little difference.

To live purposely means to choose consciously and in harmony with the Universe. Most people fail to live "purposely" because they will not consciously choose. Many live their lives out of survival and spend each day doing what they "have to do." They are masters at convincing both themselves and others that they don't have a choice. These are the people who are waiting until their retirement years to fulfill their deeper purpose. Unfortunately, many don't find their seventies or eighties much more fulfilling. A second group of people will not make a choice because they're faced with the fact that choosing one thing means un-choosing another. Although we are born with unlimited potential, we aren't born with unlimited time. These people try to be everything, and in the process master nothing. And finally, there are those who don't choose because they deeply believe that their life can't make a difference. They settle for playing small. They quit thinking about it and become intensely preoccupied with the little problems of their own life.

When you become willing to make choices in your life, your life takes on meaning. You recognize that even not making a choice has a tremendous impact on the world. Suddenly, you have a map to guide you. Decisions can be made against the backdrop of a purpose larger than your Self. Personal problems become insignificant in comparison. You recognize that you are the creator of your own life and begin to live deliberately.

An important task for parents is to help children discover their purpose. Often this is done in the process of choosing a vocation. The key for parents to remember is that children can only choose when they know they don't have to. For example, if you convince them they must choose a particular vocation in order to survive (make money, please the family, be somebody), it isn't a choice. While there may be merit in the vocation, the child will not experience meaning in it.

Parents can help their children discover purpose and choose a vocation in three ways. First (and this has been repeated throughout this book), begin telling them from infancy that they make a difference. Let them know that this is a given, and that it need not be proven to you or to anyone else. Their very existence on this planet makes a difference. Only if they get this at their very core will they be able to freely choose. Second, tell them that what they do is considerably less important than really doing what they do well. Finally, listen to your children and observe them. Discover who they really are. Your children are unique and with destinies of their own. Their interests and their timing may not coincide with your own. Ask not so much, "What would I like my child to choose?" as "What does this child need from me so that he can choose for himself?"

In conclusion, always keep in mind that a vocation is not a purpose; it's merely a form of expressing a purpose. Living purposely is more how you live than what you do.

Use every letter you write
Every conversation you have
Every meeting you attend
To express your fundamental beliefs and dreams
Affirm to others the vision of the world you want
You are a free, immensely powerful source
of life and goodness
Affirm it
Spread it
Radiate it
Think day and night about it
And you will see a miracle happen:
the greatness of your own life.

—Robert Muller
Former United Nations Assistant Secretary-General

One of the most difficult things about being
a spiritual director is to encourage people along
paths that you would not choose for yourself.

—Thérèse of Lisieux,
Story of a Soul

101

Begin It Now

Whatever you can do or dream you can, begin it.
Boldness has genius, power and magic in it.
Begin it now.

—Goethe

If this book accomplished its purpose, you have made some decisions. However, you may not have yet put these decisions into action. Some of you may be waiting for more information in the hope that someone will tell you step-by-step exactly how to do it right. Ask yourself how long you've been waiting for all the right answers, and who that gives the responsibility to anyway? Others of you haven't taken action because you're afraid of the consequences. You want guarantees that it will absolutely work as expected and that you won't feel uncomfortable, afraid, or wrong. Ask yourself what you really want. Do you want a high EQ child, or do you want to feel comfortable, secure, and right? Finally, some of you simply doubt your ability to put what you've learned into practice. Your inner critic tells you that you've already made too many mistakes and will never be able to get it right—so why try anyway? Ask yourself who you're going to listen to—the gremlins in your own mind or your inner spirit of love?

A decision that isn't followed by an action is a decision to keep things exactly as they are. Re-hashing your past, re-living your mistakes, and pondering about what you should have done creates nothing new. Thinking about change doesn't make change. If you want change you must take that crucial step from thinking to action.

For many of us, the question is where to begin. It doesn't matter. Simply ask yourself, "What do I want for my children?" Then go for it. If your intention is a loving one, you'll begin in the right place. Simply begin and do it now.

❑ Do you want to communicate more effectively?— Begin and do it now.
❑ Do you want to choose love over conflict with your teenager?—Begin and do it now.
❑ Do you want your children to know they contribute to your life?—Begin and do it now.
❑ Do you want to spend more time with your child?— Begin and do it now.
❑ Do you want to clean up your mistakes?—Begin and do it now.
❑ Do you want to give your children a spiritual basis?— Begin and do it now.
❑ Do you want to model a life of service?—Begin and do it now.

In the space below write down what you want.

Begin and do it now.

Suggested Books For Further Reading

A Path with Heart, by Jack Kornfield (New York: Bantam, 1993).

Born for Love: Reflections on Loving, by Leo F. Buscaglia (New York: Fawcett Books, 1994).

Emotional Intelligence, by Daniel Goleman, Ph.D. (New York: Bantam, 1995).

Chicken Soup for the Teenage Soul, by Jack Canfield, Mark Victor Hansen, and Kimberly Kirberger (Deerfield Beach, FL: Health Communications, Inc., 1997).

Conversations with God: An Uncommon Dialogue, by Neale Donald Walsh (New York: Putnam Publishing Group, 1996).

How Can I Help?, by Ram Dass and Paul Gorman (New York: Alfred A. Knopf, 1985).

I Will Never Leave You, by Hugh and Gayle Prather (New York: Bantam, 1995).

Just Another Spiritual Book, by Bo Lozoff (Durham, NC: Human Kindness Foundation, 1990).

Learned Optimism, by Martin E. P. Seligman, Ph.D. (New York: Simon & Schuster, 1990).

People are Just Desserts, by Perry Arledge (Austin, TX: Perry Productions).

Random Acts of Kindness, by the Editors of Conari Press (Berkeley, CA: Conari Press, 1993).

Teaching Your Children Values, by Linda and Richard Eyre (New York: Simon & Schuster, 1993).

The Moral Intelligence of Children, by Robert Coles, M.D. (New York: Random House, 1997).

The Road Less Traveled, by M. Scott Peck, M.D. (New York: Simon & Schuster, 1978).

Winning Through Enlightenment, by Ron Smothermon, M.D. (San Francisco: Context Publications, 1982).

About The Authors

Allen and Geraldine Nagy have many years of experience promoting the well-being of people from every walk of life. They are experts in the fields of holistic health, psychospirituality, professional development, and emotional intelligence.

Allen is an inspiring speaker and author. He holds a Ph.D. in counseling, and has over twenty years of experience as a Chief Psychologist and Drug Abuse Program Coordinator in three Federal Penitentiaries and one correctional institution. He was creator of the first Holistic Health Program in the Federal system, which specifically addressed the lack of emotional intelligence as a primary contributor to criminality. This program has been used as a model for other institutions, and has been described in *Omni* magazine and other publications because of his optimistic perspective on rehabilitation and making a difference in the lives of others.

Geraldine is a captivating speaker and author as well. She received her Ph.D. in psychology with ground-breaking publications in the areas of organizational decision making and human judgement. She has spoken for organizations throughout the U.S.A. and South America. Her keynote addresses and seminars are noted for their high energy, spontaneous humor, and participant involvement. Her work has been featured in *Random Acts of Kindness* by Conari Press.

Both Geraldine and Allen view life as a choice between peace and conflict, and love and fear. They believe that Humankind cannot reach its fullest potential unless we all awaken to this choice. Their paths in Life are to assist others to awaken along with them.

They have been married for 30 years and have one son, Clint, who is 21 years old. They live among the beautiful "lost pines" in Bastrop, Texas.

How To Reach Us

We would like to hear from you regarding your experiences in raising the Emotional Intelligence of your children. Please send your success stories or comments to:

> **Allen/Geraldine Nagy, Ph.D.**
> **Heartfelt Publications**
> **P.O. Box 1090**
> **Bastrop, TX 78602**
> **Tel: 1-800-892-7006 Fax: 512-332-0874**
> **E-mail: heartfelt@ibm.net**
> **Web: www.heartfeltpublications.com**

Geraldine and Allen are professional speakers and provide a variety of programs relating to Emotional Intelligence at home, in the schools, and in the workplace.

For businesses and corporations, we offer seminars on Managerial EQ, conflict resolution, managing change, communication skills, and our unique leadership course called *Power Tools*

For individuals/families we offer a 1-day relationships course; a 2-day program called *Powerful Beyond Belief: The Art Of Purposeful Living*, and a 2-day program designed especially for adolescents called *GET SMART*.

We are available for key-note presentations on Emotional Intelligence and the Art of Living Purposely.

If you would like more information about any of these programs, please call us or send your name, company name (if applicable), and telephone number to us and we will contact you.

- ♦ Keynote speaking
- ♦ In-service training for educators and school counselors
- ♦ Half-day or full-day on-site leadership training programs
- ♦ Our two-day *Power Tools* program for managers
- ♦ Our two-day *Powerful Beyond Belief* program
- ♦ Our two-day *Get Smart* program for adolescents
- ♦ Personal telephone consultations
- ♦ Individualized coaching/mentoring programs

Notes:

Notes:

Notes:

Notes:

Notes:

Notes:

Notes:

Notes:

Notes:

Notes:

Ordering Our Book

Parents and their children hold a special place within our hearts. It has been our intention to inspire you, remind you that you make a difference, and give you something that you can use. If we have been successful and you have found value in this book, please share it with everyone that you know. If you know others who might like to order a book of their own, please pass this order form on to them.

HOW TO RAISE YOUR CHILD'S
EMOTIONAL INTELLIGENCE:
101 Ways To Bring Out The Best In Your Children And Yourself
by Allen Nagy, Ph.D. and Geraldine Nagy, Ph.D.

May be ordered through:

Heartfelt Publications
P.O. Box 1090
Bastrop, TX 78602
TEL: 1-800-892-7006   **FAX: 512-332-0874**
E-mail: heartfelt@ibm.net

QTY_____ at $14.95 each......................._____
Texas residents add 8% sales tax............._____
Shipping first book, $2..........................._____
Shipping each additional book, $0.50......._____
                                        Total:_____

Send to:
Name:_____
Street:_____
City:_____ State:_____ Zip:_____

Ordering Our Book

Parents and their children hold a special place within our hearts. It has been our intention to inspire you, remind you that you make a difference, and give you something that you can use. If we have been successful and you have found value in this book, please share it with everyone that you know. If you know others who might like to order a book of their own, please pass this order form on to them.

HOW TO RAISE YOUR CHILD'S EMOTIONAL INTELLIGENCE:
101 Ways To Bring Out The Best In Your Children And Yourself
by Allen Nagy, Ph.D. and Geraldine Nagy, Ph.D.

May be ordered through:

Heartfelt Publications
P.O. Box 1090
Bastrop, TX 78602
TEL: 1-800-892-7006   FAX: 512-332-0874
E-mail: heartfelt@ibm.net

QTY_____ at $14.95 each......................._____

Texas residents add 8% sales tax............._____

Shipping first book, $2............................_____

Shipping each additional book, $0.50......._____

                              Total:_____

Send to:

Name:_____

Street:_____

City:_____ State:_____ Zip:_____